STUDENTS' GUIDE TO PROGRAM DESIGN

Lesley Anne Robertson

Lecturer in Computing
University of Western Sydney

NEWNES

To David, Lucy and Sally

Newnes
An imprint of Butterworth-Heinemann Ltd
Linacre House, Jordan Hill, Oxford OX2 8DP

PART OF REED INTERNATIONAL BOOKS

OXFORD LONDON BOSTON
MUNICH NEW DELHI SINGAPORE SYDNEY
TOKYO TORONTO WELLINGTON

First published by Thomas Nelson Australia 1989
Reprinted 1990

First published in Great Britain 1992

British Library Cataloguing in Publication Data
A catalogue record for this book is available from the British Library

ISBN 0 7506 0495 6

Composition by Genesis Typesetting, Laser Quay, Rochester, Kent
Printed and bound in Great Britain by
Biddles Ltd, Guildford and King's Lynn

CONTENTS

3 Developing an algorithm 18

This chapter introduces methods of analyzing a problem and developing a solution. Simple algorithms which use the sequence control structure are developed, and methods of manually checking the algorithm are determined.

4 Selection control structures 35

This chapter expands the selection control structure by introducing multiple selection, nested selection, and the *case* construct in solution algorithms. Several algorithms, using variations of the selection control structure, are developed.

5 Repetition control structures 56

This chapter develops algorithms which use the repetition control structure in the form of DOWHILE, REPEAT..UNTIL, and counted repetition loops.

6 Pseudocode algorithms using sequence, selection and repetition 78

This chapter develops algorithms to eight simple programming problems, which use combinations of sequence, selection and repetition constructs. Each problem is properly defined; the control structures required are established; a pseudocode algorithm is developed; and the solution is manually checked for logic errors.

7 Modularization 94

This chapter introduces modularization as a means of dividing a problem into subtasks. Hierarchy charts are introduced as a pictorial representation of program module structure. Several algorithms which use a modular structure are developed.

8 Module design considerations 114

This chapter introduces the concepts of module cohesion, inter-module communication, local and global data, scope, side effects, and the passing of parameters between modules. Several levels of cohesion and coupling are described and pseudocode examples of each level are provided.

This chapter develops a general pseudocode algorithm for five common business applications. All problems are defined; a hierarchy chart is established; and a pseudocode algorithm is developed, using a mainline and several subordinate modules. The problems covered include report generation with page break, a single-level control break, a multiple-level control break, a sequential file update program and array processing.

A revision of the steps a programmer must follow to achieve good program design.

PREFACE

With the increased popularity of programming courses in our universities, colleges and technical institutions, a need has arisen for an easy to read textbook on program design. There are already dozens of introductory programming texts using specific languages such as PASCAL, BASIC or COBOL. These texts, however, usually gloss over the important step of designing a solution to a given programming problem. Program design can be described as the development of a solution algorithm, independent of language, which will be used for translation into a specific programming language. Designing this algorithm is seen as developing the framework of the solution.

This textbook tackles the subject of program design by using structured programming techniques and pseudocode to develop a solution algorithm. The actual pseudocode recommended in the book has been chosen because of its closeness to written English and to the syntax of most structured programming languages.

In the earlier chapters, Nassi–Schneiderman diagrams have been presented alongside pseudocode to illustrate a more visual method of algorithm representation. In the later chapters, only pseudocode algorithms are developed, as pseudocode is more versatile, and easier to manipulate than Nassi–Schneiderman diagrams.

Simple Program Design is designed for beginner programmers who want to develop the programming skills necessary to solve common business problems. Too often, programmers, when faced with a problem, launch straight into the code of their chosen programming language, instead of concentrating on the actual problem at hand. They become bogged down with the syntax and format of the language, and often spend many hours getting the program to work. Using this textbook, the programmer will learn how to define the problem; how to design a solution algorithm; and how to prove the algorithm's *correctness,* before coding a single word from any programming language. By using pseudocode and structured techniques the programmer can concentrate on developing a well designed and correct solution, and thus eliminate many frustrating hours at the testing phase.

This textbook has been divided into ten chapters, beginning with a basic explanation of structured programming techniques, top-down development and modular design. Then, concept by concept, the student is introduced to the *syntax* of pseudocode; methods of defining the problem; the application of basic control structures in the development of the solution algorithm; desk checking techniques; hierarchy charts; and module design considerations.

Each chapter thoroughly covers the topic at hand, giving practical examples relating to business applications, and a consistently structured approach when representing algorithms and hierarchy charts.

CHAPTER 1

PROGRAM DESIGN

Objectives

- To describe the steps in the program development process
- To explain structured programming
- To introduce algorithms and pseudocode

Outline

1.1 Steps in program development

1.2 Structured programming

1.3 An introduction to algorithms and pseudocode

1.4 Chapter summary

1.1 Steps in program development

Computer programming is an art. Many people believe that a programmer must be good at mathematics, must have a memory for figures and technical information, and must be prepared to spend many hours sitting at a terminal, typing in programs. However, given the right tools, and steps to follow, anyone can write programs. It is a task worth doing, as it is both stimulating and fulfilling.

Programming can be defined as the development of a solution to an identified problem, and the setting up of a related series of instructions, which, when directed through computer hardware, will produce the desired results. It is the first part of this definition which satisfies the programmer's creative needs, ie to design a solution to an identified problem. Yet this step is so often overlooked. The practice of leaping straight into the coding phase without first designing a proper solution usually results in programs that contain a lot of errors. Often the programmer needs to spend a significant amount of time finding these errors and correcting them. A more experienced programmer will design a solution to the program first, desk check this solution, and then code the program into a chosen programming language.

There are seven basic steps in the development of a program and these will be described in detail throughout the next few chapters. An outline of these seven steps follows:

1 Define the problem

This step involves the careful reading, and re-reading of the problem until the programmer understands completely what is required.

2 Outline the solution

Once the problem has been defined, the programmer may decide to break the problem up into smaller tasks or steps, and several solutions may be considered. The solution outline often takes the shape of a hierarchy or structure chart.

3 Develop the outline into an algorithm

Using the solution outline developed in Step 2, the programmer then expands this into a set of precise steps which describe exactly the tasks to be performed and the order in which they are to be carried out. This step uses both structured programming techniques and pseudocode.

4 Test the algorithm for correctness

This step is one of the most important in the development of a program, and yet it is the step most often forgotten. Test data needs to be *walked through* each step in the algorithm to check that the instructions described in the algorithm will actually do what they are supposed to. If logic errors are discovered then they can be easily corrected.

5 Code the algorithm into a specific programming language

It is only after all design considerations have been met in the previous four steps that the programmer actually starts to code the program.

6 Run the program on the computer

This step uses a program compiler and programmer-designed test data to machine test the code for both syntax and logic errors. This is usually the most rewarding step in the program development process. If the program has been well designed then the usual time-wasting frustration and despair often associated with program testing are reduced to a minimum. This step may need to be performed several times until the programmer is satisfied that the program is running as required.

7 Document and maintain the program

Program documentation should not be listed as the last step in the program development process, as it is really an ongoing task from the initial definition of the problem to the final test result.

Documentation involves both external documentation, such as hierarchy charts, the solution algorithm, and test data results; and internal documentation coded in the program. Program maintenance refers to changes which may need to be made to a program throughout its life. Often these changes are performed by a different programmer from the one who initially wrote the program. If the program has been well designed using structured programming techniques, then the code will be seen as self documenting, resulting in greater ease of maintenance.

1.2 Structured programming

Structured programming assists the programmer to write effective error-free programs. The original concept of structured programming was devised in a paper published in 1964 in Italy by Böhm and Jacopini. This paper established the idea of using a theorem based on three control structures when designing programs. Since then, a number of authors such as Edsger Dijkstra, Niklaus Wirth, Ed Yourdon and Michael Jackson have developed the original concept further and have contributed to the establishment of the popular term *structured programming*. This term now refers not only to the Structure Theorem itself, but also *top-down development* and *modular design*.

Top-down development

Traditionally, a programmer, when presented with a programming problem, would start coding at the beginning and work systematically through each step until reaching the end. Often the programmer would get bogged down in the intricacies of a particular part of the problem, rather than considering the solution as a whole. In the top-down development of a program design, a general solution to the problem is outlined first. This is then broken down gradually into more detailed steps until finally the most detailed levels have been completed. It is only after this process of *stepwise refinement* that the programmer starts to code. The result of this systematic, disciplined approach to program design, is a higher precision programming than possible before.

Modular design

Structured programming also incorporates the concept of modular design which involves grouping tasks together because they all perform the same function, eg the calculation of sales tax, or the printing of report headings. Modular design is connected directly to top-down development, as the steps or subtasks which the programmer breaks up the program solution into, will actually form the future modules of the program. Good modular design aids in the reading and understanding of the program.

The Structure Theorem

The Structure Theorem revolutionized program design by both eliminating the GOTO statement, and establishing a structured framework for representing the solution. The Theorem states that it is possible to write any computer program by using only three basic control structures. These control structures are:

1 Sequence
2 Selection, or IF-THEN-ELSE, and
3 Repetition, or DOWHILE

These control structures will be covered in detail in Chapter 2.

1.3 An introduction to algorithms and pseudocode

Structured programming techniques require a program to be properly designed before coding begins, and it is this design process which results in the construction of an algorithm.

What is an algorithm?

An algorithm is like a recipe. It lists the steps involved in accomplishing a task. It can be defined in programming terms as a set of detailed, unambiguous and ordered instructions developed to describe the processes necessary to produce the desired output from the given input. The algorithm is written in simple English and is not a formalized procedure. However, to be useful, there are some principles which should be adhered to. An algorithm must:

1 be lucid, precise and unambiguous,
2 give the correct solution in all cases, and
3 eventually end.

For example, if you want to instruct someone to add up a list of prices on a pocket calculator, you might write an algorithm like the following:

```
Turn on calculator
Clear calculator

Repeat the following instructions
   Key in pounds amount
   Key in decimal point (.)
   Key in pence amount
   Press plus (+) key
Until all prices have been entered

Press equal (=) key
Write down total price
Turn off calculator
```

Notice that in this algorithm the first two steps are performed once, before the repetitive process of entering the prices. After all the prices have been entered and summed, the solution is obtained by pressing the equal key and writing down the total price. These final two activities and the turning off of the calculator are also performed only once. This algorithm satisfies the desired list of properties. It lists all the steps in the correct order from top to bottom, in a definite and unambiguous fashion until a correct solution is reached. Notice that the steps to be repeated, the entering and summing of the prices, are indented, both to separate them from those steps performed only once, and to emphasize the repetitive nature of their action. It is important to use indentation when writing solution algorithms. Indentation helps to differentiate between the three control structures.

What is pseudocode?

Traditionally, flowcharts were used to represent the steps in an algorithm diagrammatically. However, they were found to be bulky, difficult to draw and often led to poor program structure. In contrast, pseudocode is easy to read and write, as it represents the statements of an algorithm in English. Pseudocode is really structured English. It is English which has been formalized and abbreviated to look very like high level computer languages.

There is currently no standard pseudocode. Textbook authors seem to adopt their own special techniques and set of rules which often resemble a particular programming language. This book will attempt to establish a *standard* pseudocode for use by all programmers, regardless of the programming language they choose. Like many versions of pseudocode this *standard* version has certain conventions, as follows:

1 Statements are written in simple English.
2 Each instruction is written on a separate line.
3 Keywords and indentation are used to signify particular control structures.
4 Each set of instructions is written from top to bottom with only one entry and one exit.
5 Groups of statements may be formed into modules, and that group given a name.

Pseudocode has been chosen to represent the solution algorithms in this book because its use allows the programmer to concentrate on the logic of the problem.

However, in the earlier chapters, Nassi–Schneiderman diagrams also appear alongside the pseudocode, for those beginner programmers who prefer a more pictorial method of representing algorithms. Nassi–Schneiderman diagrams and pseudocode are described in detail in the next chapter.

1.4 Chapter summary

In this chapter, the steps in program development were introduced and briefly described. These seven steps were: define the problem, outline the solution, develop the outline into an algorithm, test the algorithm for correctness, code the algorithm into a specific programming language, run the program on the computer and document and maintain the program.

Structured programming was presented as a combination of three separate concepts: top-down development, modular design, and the use of the Structure Theorem when designing a solution to a problem. All these concepts will be developed further with examples.

An algorithm was defined as a set of detailed, unambiguous and ordered instructions developed to describe the processes necessary to produce the desired output from the given input. Pseudocode is an English-like form of representation of the algorithm and its advantages, and some conventions for its use, were listed.

CHAPTER 2

PSEUDOCODE AND NASSI–SCHNEIDERMAN DIAGRAMS

Objectives

- To introduce common words and keywords used when writing pseudocode
- To define the three basic control structures as set out in the Structure Theorem
- To illustrate the three basic control structures using pseudocode and Nassi–Schneiderman diagrams

Outline

2.1 How to write pseudocode

2.2 The Structure Theorem

2.3 Chapter summary

2.1 How to write pseudocode

When designing a solution algorithm, a programmer needs to keep in mind that the set of instructions will eventually be performed by a computer. That is, if the programmer uses words and phrases in his or her pseudocode which are in line with basic computer operations, then the translation from the pseudocode algorithm to a specific programming language becomes quite simple.

This chapter establishes six basic computer operations and introduces common words and keywords which are used to represent these operations in pseudocode. Each operation can be represented as a straightforward English instruction, with keywords and indentation to signify a particular control structure.

Six basic computer operations

1 A computer can receive information

When a computer is required to receive information or input from a particular source, whether it be a terminal, a disk or any other device, the verbs *Read* and *Get* are used in pseudocode. For example typical pseudocode instructions to receive information are:

```
Read student name
Get system date
Read number1, number2
```

Each example uses a single verb, *Read* or *Get,* followed by one or more nouns to indicate what data is required to be obtained. At no stage is it necessary to specify the source of the data as this information is not required until run time.

2 A computer can put out information

When a computer is required to supply information or output to a device the verbs *Print, Write* or *Put* are used in pseudocode. Typical pseudocode examples are:

```
Print student number
Write 'Program Completed'
Write customer record to master file
Put out name, address and postcode
```

In each example, the data to be written out is described concisely using mostly lower case letters.

3 A computer can perform arithmetic

Most programs require the computer to perform some sort of mathematical calculation, or formula, and for these, a programmer may either use actual mathematical symbols, or the words for those symbols. For instance, the same pseudocode instruction can be expressed as:

```
Add Number to Total
            or
Total = Total + Number
```

Both expressions clearly instruct the computer to add one value to another and, therefore, either are acceptable in pseudocode. The equal symbol, '=', has been used to indicate *assignment* of a value, as a result of some processing.

To keep in line with high level programming languages, the following symbols can be written in pseudocode:

+ for Add
- for Subtract
* for Multiply
/ for Divide
() for Brackets

The verbs *compute* and *calculate* are also available. Some pseudocode examples to perform a calculation are:

```
Divide Totalmarks by Studentcount
VAT = Costprice * 0.175
Compute C = (F – 32) * 5/9
```

4 A computer can assign a value to a piece of data

There are many cases where a programmer may need to assign a value to a piece of information. Firstly, to give data an initial value in pseudocode the verbs *Initialize* or *Set* are used. Secondly, to assign a value as a result of some processing, the symbol '=' is written. Thirdly, to keep a piece of information for later use, the verbs *Save* or *Store* are used. Some typical pseudocode examples are:

```
Initialize total accumulators to zero
Set Studentcount to 0
Totalprice = Costprice + VAT
Store Customernum in Lastcustomernum
```

5 A computer can compare two pieces of information and select one of two alternative actions

An important computer operation available to the programmer is the ability to compare two pieces of information, and then, as a result of the comparison, select one of two alternative actions. To represent this operation in pseudocode, special keywords are used, viz IF, THEN and ELSE. The comparison of data is established in the IF clause, and the choice of alternatives is determined by the THEN or ELSE options. Only one of these alternatives will be performed. A typical pseudocode example to illustrate this operation is:

```
IF student is parttime THEN
   add 1 to parttimecount
ELSE
   add 1 to fulltimecount
ENDIF
```

In this example the attendance pattern of the student is investigated, with the result that either the parttimecount, or fulltimecount accumulator is incremented. Note the use of indentation to emphasize the THEN and ELSE options, and the use of the delimiter ENDIF, to close the operation.

6 A computer can repeat a group of actions

When there is a sequence of processing steps which need to be repeated, two special keywords DOWHILE and ENDDO are used in pseudocode. The condition for the repetition of a group of actions is established in the DOWHILE clause, and the actions to be repeated are listed beneath it. For example:

```
DOWHILE studenttotal < 50
   Read student record
   Write student name, address to report
   Add 1 to Studenttotal
ENDDO
```

In this example, it is easy to see the statements which are to be repeated, as they immediately follow the DOWHILE statement, and are indented for added emphasis. The condition which controls, and eventually terminates the repetition is established in the DOWHILE clause, and the keyword ENDDO acts as a delimiter. As soon as the condition for repetition is found to be false, control passes to the next statement after the ENDDO.

Other texts may use the keywords WHILE and ENDWHILE to start and end this operation, however the format and function of the pseudocode is the same.

2.2 The Structure Theorem

The Structure Theorem forms the basic framework for structured programming. It states that it is possible to write any computer program by using only three basic control structures, viz:

1 sequence
2 selection, and
3 repetition.

These control structures are easily represented in pseudocode and Nassi–Schneiderman diagrams.

The three basic control structures

1 Sequence

The sequence control structure is defined as the straightforward execution of one processing step after another. In pseudocode, we represent this construct as a sequence of pseudocode statements:

```
Statement a
Statement b
Statement c
```

A Nassi–Schneiderman (N–S) diagram represents this control structure as a series of rectangular boxes, one beneath the other:

Statement a
Statement b
Statement c

The sequence control structure can be used to represent the first four basic computer operations listed previously. These operations can receive information, put out information, perform arithmetic and assign values. For example a typical sequence of statements in an algorithm might read:

```
Add 1 to Pagecount
Write Heading Line
Set Linecount to zero
Read customer record
```

These same statements in a N–S diagram would read:

Add 1 to Pagecount
Write Heading Line
Set Linecount to zero
Read customer record

These instructions illustrate the sequence control structure as a straightforward list of steps, written one after the other, in a top to bottom fashion. Each instruction will be executed in the order in which it appears.

2 Selection

The selection control structure can be defined as the presentation of a condition, and the choice between two actions depending on whether the condition is true or false. This construct represents the decision making abilities of the computer and is used to illustrate the fifth basic computer operation.

In pseudocode, selection is represented by the keywords IF, THEN, ELSE and ENDIF:

```
IF condition p is true THEN
   statement(s) in true case
ELSE
   statement(s) in false case
ENDIF
```

Basically if condition p is true then the statement or statements in the true case will be executed, and the statements in the false case will be skipped. Otherwise, (the else statement) the statements in the true case will be skipped and statements in the false case will be executed. Control then passes to the next processing step after the delimiter ENDIF.

A N–S diagram represents the selection control structure pictorially as the testing of a condition which can lead to two separate paths:

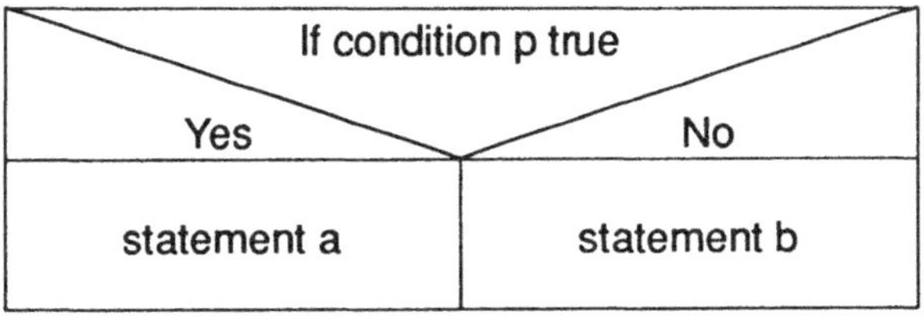

If condition p is true the statement or statements in the *yes* box will be executed. If condition p is false, the statement or statements in the *no* box will be executed. Both paths then lead to the next box following the selection control structure.

A typical pseudocode example might read:

```
IF student is parttime THEN
   add 1 to parttimecount
ELSE
   add 1 to fulltimecount
ENDIF
```

The same logic in a N–S diagram would look like this:

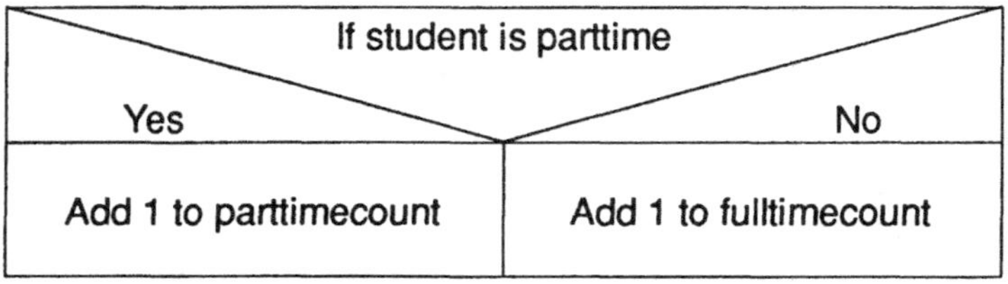

A variation of the selection control structure is the null ELSE structure, which is used when a task is performed only if a particular condition is true. The null ELSE construct is written in pseudocode as:

```
IF condition p is true THEN
   statement(s) in true case
ENDIF
```

Note, the keyword ELSE is omitted. This construct tests the condition in the IF clause and if found to be true, performs the statement or statements listed in the THEN clause. However, if the initial condition is found to be false, then no action will be taken and processing will proceed to the next statement after the ENDIF.

The N–S diagram which represents the null ELSE construct simply leaves the *No* box blank, or includes the words *No action* in that box.

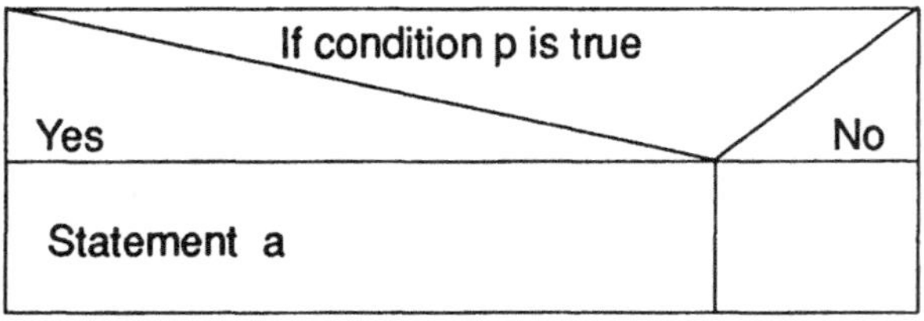

3 Repetition

The repetition control structure can be defined as the presentation of a set of instructions to be performed repeatedly, as long as a condition is true. The basic idea of repetitive code is that a block of statements is executed again and again, until a terminating condition occurs. This construct represents the sixth basic computer operation and is written in pseudocode as:

```
DOWHILE condition p is true
   statement block
ENDDO
```

The DOWHILE loop is a leading decision loop, that is, the condition is tested before any statements are executed. If the condition in the DOWHILE statement is found to be true, then the block of statements following that statement is executed once. The delimiter ENDDO then triggers a return of control to the retesting of the condition. If the condition is still true, then the statements are repeated, and so the repetition process continues until the condition is found to be false. Control then passes to the statement which follows the ENDDO statement. It is imperative that at least one statement within the statement block can alter the condition, and eventually render it false, otherwise the logic will result in an endless loop.

A N–S diagram represents this structure as one rectangular box inside an L-shaped frame:

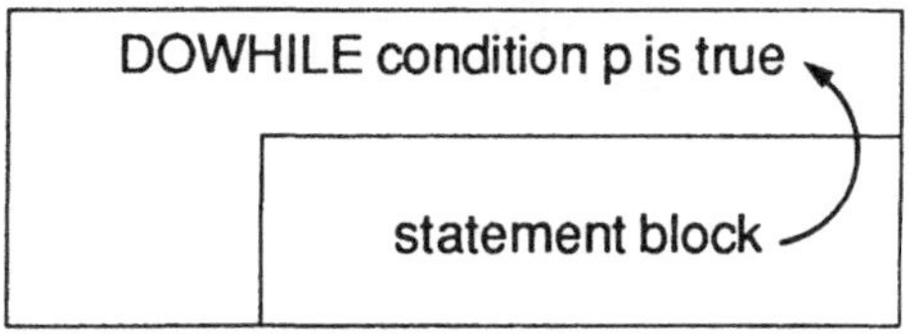

While condition p is true, the statements inside the rectangular box will be executed. The last line of the box acts as the delimiter, and returns control to retest condition p (see up arrow). When condition p is false control will pass out of the repetition structure down the false path to the next statement (see down arrow).

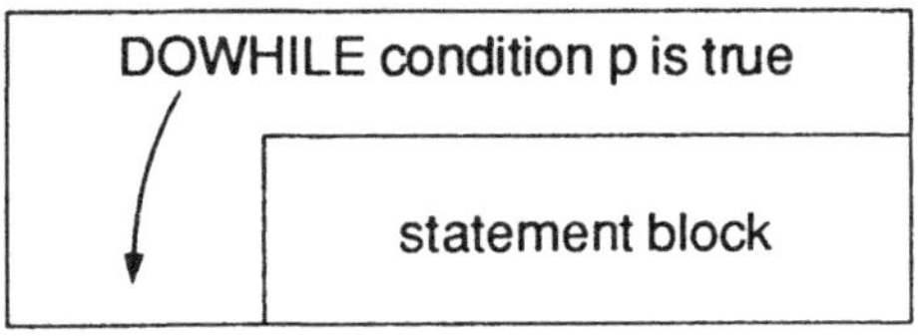

We will now look at a pseudocode example which represents the repetition control structure:

```
Set studenttotal to zero
DOWHILE studenttotal < 50
   Read student record
   Write student name, address to report
   Add 1 to studenttotal
ENDDO
```

This example illustrates a number of points:

1 The variable studenttotal is initialized before the DOWHILE condition is executed.
2 As long as studenttotal is less than 50, (ie the DOWHILE condition is true) then the statement block will be repeated.
3 Each time the statement block is executed, one instruction within that block will cause the variable studenttotal to be incremented.
4 After 50 iterations, studenttotal will equal 50, which causes the DOWHILE condition to become false and the repetition to cease.

It is important to realize that the initializing and subsequent incrementation of the variable tested in the condition is an essential feature of the DOWHILE construct.

The same algorithm can be represented in a N–S diagram as follows:

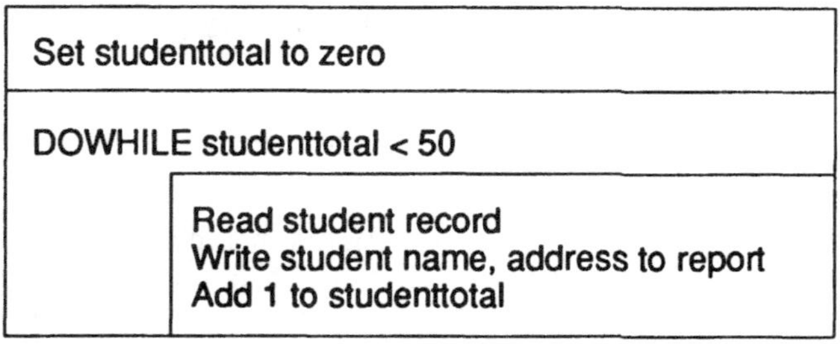

N–S diagrams are very similar to pseudocode. They simply offer a more diagrammatic approach for those programmers who prefer a visual method of representation.

2.3 Chapter summary

In this chapter, six basic computer operations were listed, along with pseudocode words and keywords to represent them. These operations were: to receive information, put out information, perform arithmetic, assign a value to a piece of data, decide between two alternate actions and repeat a group of actions. Typical pseudocode examples were given as illustrations.

The Structure Theorem was introduced. It states that it is possible to write any computer program by using only three basic control structures, viz sequence, selection and repetition. Each control structure was defined, and its association with each of the six basic computer operations was indicated. Pseudocode examples and Nassi–Schneiderman diagrams for each control structure were provided.

CHAPTER 3

DEVELOPING AN ALGORITHM

Objectives

- To introduce methods of analyzing a problem and developing a solution
- To develop simple algorithms using the sequence control structure
- To introduce methods of manually checking the developed solution

Outline

3.1 Defining the problem

3.2 Designing a solution algorithm

3.3 Checking the solution algorithm

3.4 Chapter summary

3.5 Programming problems

3.1 Defining the problem

In Chapter 1 it was established that there are seven steps in the development of a computer program. The very first step, and one of the most important, is the defining of the problem. This involves the careful reading and re-reading of the problem until the programmer understands completely what is required. Quite often, additional information will need to be sought to fill out ambiguities or deficiencies in the problem specification. As an aid in this initial analysis, the problem should be divided into three separate components:

1 Input, or source data provided to the problem;
2 Output, or end result, which is required to be produced;
3 Processing, or a list of what actions are required to be performed.

When reading the problem statement, the input and output components are easily identified as they are expressed using descriptive words, such as nouns and adjectives. The processing component is also identified easily. The problem statement usually describes the processing steps as actions, using verbs and adverbs. When dividing a problem into its three different components, a programmer should simply analyze the actual words used in the specification, and divide them into those which are descriptive, and those which imply actions. It may be helpful to underline the nouns and verbs used in the specification to help in this process. The processing section at this stage should be a list of *what* actions need to be performed, not *how* they will be accomplished. The programmer should not attempt to find a solution until the problem has been completely defined. Let's look at a simple example.

Example 3.1 Add three numbers

A program is required to read three numbers, add them together, and print their total.

This problem should be tackled in two stages. Firstly, the programmer should underline the nouns and adjectives used in the specification. This will establish the input and output components of the problem, as well as any other objects which are required. With the nouns and adjectives underlined, our example would look like this:

A program is required to read <u>three numbers</u>, add them together, and print their <u>total</u>.

By looking at the underlined nouns and adjectives, it can be seen that the input for this problem is *three numbers* and the output, the *total*.

It is helpful to write down these first two components in a simple diagram. This diagram will be called a *defining diagram.*

INPUT	*PROCESSING*	*OUTPUT*
Three numbers		Total

Having established the input and output components the programmer should now underline the verbs and adverbs used in the specification. This will establish the actions required to be performed. Example 3.1 should now look like this:

A program is required to read three numbers, add them together, and print their total.

By looking at the underlined words, it can be seen that the processing verbs are *read, add together* and *print*. These steps can now be added to our defining diagram to make it complete. Note that when writing down each processing verb the objects or nouns associated with each verb should also be included. The defining diagram now becomes:

INPUT	*PROCESSING*	*OUTPUT*
Three numbers	Read three numbers Add numbers together Print total number	Total

Now that all the nouns and verbs in the specification have been considered, and the defining diagram is complete, it could be said that the problem has been properly defined. That is, the programmer now understands the input to the problem, the output to be produced, and the processing steps required to convert the input to the output.

Meaningful names

At this stage it is a good idea to introduce some unique names which will be used both to represent the variables or objects in the problem, and to describe the processing steps. All names should be meaningful. A name given to a variable is simply a method of identifying a particular storage location in the computer. The uniqueness of the name will differentiate it from other locations. The name itself should be transparent enough to adequately describe the variable. For instance, Number1, Number2 and Number3 are more meaningful names for the numbers in our example, Add three numbers, than A, B and C.

When it comes to writing down the processing component, a programmer should use words which describe the work to be done as single specific tasks or functions. In the above example the processing steps were written down as verbs accompanied by their associated objects:

Read three numbers
Add numbers together
Print total number

There is a pattern in the words chosen to describe these steps. Each action is described as a single verb followed by a two word object. Studies have shown that if a programmer follows this convention to describe a processing step, then two benefits will result. Firstly, the programmer is using a disciplined approach to defining the problem and secondly, the processing is being dissected into separate tasks or functions. This simple operation of dividing a problem into separate functions, and choosing a proper name for each function becomes extremely important, later, when considering modules.

Example 3.2 Find average temperature

A program is required to read in the maximum and minimum temperatures on a particular day and calculate and print the average temperature.

First let's establish the input and output components by underlining the nouns and adjectives in the problem statement.

A program is required to read in the maximum and minimum temperatures on a particular day and calculate and print the average temperature.

The input component is the *maximum and minimum temperatures* and the output is the *average temperature.* Using meaningful names, these components can be set up in a defining diagram:

INPUT	*PROCESSING*	*OUTPUT*
Max-temp Min-temp		Avg-temp

Now establish the processing steps, by underlining the verbs and adverbs in the problem statement.

A program is required to read in the maximum and minimum temperatures on a particular day and calculate and print the average temperature.

The processing verbs are *read, calculate* and *print*. By finding the associated objects of these verbs, the defining diagram can now be completed, as follows:

INPUT	PROCESSING	OUTPUT
Max-temp	Read max, min temperatures	Avg-temp
Min-temp	Calculate average temperature	
	Print average temperature	

Remember that at this stage the programmer is not concerned with *how* the average temperature will be calculated. That will come later, when the solution algorithm is established.

Example 3.3 Calculate coin denominations

A program is required to read in an amount of a purchase in pence which is not to exceed one pound. The change from one pound is then to be calculated and printed as the most compact set of change (ie the fewest coins). It is assumed that the denominations available are 50p, 20p, 10p, 5p, 2p and 1p.

To establish the input and output components in this problem, the nouns and adjectives have been underlined. By reading these words, it can be seen that the input is *an amount of a purchase in pence,* and the output is *the most compact set of change.* Other nouns such as *fewest coins* and *denominations available* do not constitute separate objects, but are necessary to establish the exact meaning of *most compact set of change.* The actual denominations (50p, 20p, etc) are also given to clarify the problem, and will be used as variables in the solution algorithm.

The input and output components can be set up in a defining diagram as follows:

INPUT	PROCESSING	OUTPUT
Pence-amount		Set-of-change

Now the verbs and adverbs in the problem statement can be underlined.

A program is required to read in an amount of a purchase in pence, which is not to exceed one pound. The change from one pound is then to be calculated and printed as the most compact set of change (ie the fewest coins). It is assumed that the denominations available are 50p, 20p, 10p, 5p, 2p and 1p.

The processing steps can now be added to the defining diagram as follows:

INPUT	*PROCESSING*	*OUTPUT*
Pence-amount	Read purchase amount Calculate change from £1.00 Calculate set of change Print set of change	Set-of-change

The four steps listed in the defining diagram are sufficient to establish the requirements of the problem. The programmer must be absolutely confident of *what* is to be done in the program, before he or she can attempt to establish *how*.

3.2 Designing a solution algorithm

Designing a solution algorithm is the most challenging task in the life cycle of a program. Once the program has been properly defined, the programmer usually begins with a *rough sketch* of the steps required to solve the problem. He or she will look at *what* is required and, using these requirements and the three basic control structures defined in the Structure Theorem, will attempt to establish *how* the processing will take place.

Usually the first attempt at designing an algorithm does not result in a finished product. Steps may be left out, or some that are included may later be altered or deleted. Pseudocode is useful in this trial and error process, since it is relatively easy to add, delete, or alter an instruction. A programmer should not hesitate to alter algorithms or even discard one and start again, if it is not completely satisfactory. If the algorithm is not correct, then the program will never be.

There is some argument that the work of a *programmer* ends with the algorithm design. After that, a *coder*, or trainee programmer could take over and code the solution algorithm into a specific programming language. In practice, this usually doesn't happen. However it should be emphasized that programmers should not be too anxious to start coding until the necessary steps of defining the problem and designing the solution algorithm have been completed.

Let us now look at solution algorithms for the preceding three examples. All involve sequence control structures only; there are no decisions or loops, and so they are relatively easy.

Example 3.1 Add three numbers

A program is required to read three numbers, add them together and print their total.

a Defining diagram

INPUT	*PROCESSING*	*OUTPUT*
Number1	Read three numbers	Total
Number2	Add numbers together	
Number3	Print total number	

This diagram shows *what* is required, and a simple calculation will establish *how*. Using pseudocode, and the sequence control structure, the solution algorithm can be established as follows:

b Solution algorithm

```
Add-Three-Numbers
    Read Number1, Number2, Number3
    Total = Number1 + Number2 + Number3
    Print Total
END
```

There are a number of points to consider in this solution algorithm:

1 A name has been given to the algorithm. The name should briefly describe the function of the algorithm, and is usually expressed as a single verb followed by a two-word object. Other names which are equally suitable could be 'Process-Three-Numbers' and 'Total-Three-Numbers'.
2 An 'END' statement at the end of the algorithm indicates that the algorithm is complete.
3 All processing steps between the algorithm name and the END statement have been indented for readability (usually two spaces).
4 Each processing step in the defining diagram relates directly to a statement (or statements) in the algorithm. For instance, 'Read three numbers' in the defining diagram becomes 'Read Number1, Number2, Number3' in the algorithm; and 'Add numbers together' becomes 'Total = Number1 + Number2 + Number3'.

Now that the algorithm is complete, the programmer should *desk check* the solution, and then translate it into a chosen programming language. Desk checking will be covered later in this chapter.

A N–S diagram could have been used to express the solution algorithm to Example 3.1 as follows:

Add-Three-Numbers

Read Number1, Number2, Number3
Total = Number1 + Number2 + Number3
Print Total

Example 3.2 Find average temperature

A program is required to read in the maximum and minimum temperatures on a particular day, and calculate and print the average temperature.

a Defining diagram

INPUT	*PROCESSING*	*OUTPUT*
Max-temp	Read max, min temperatures	Avg-temp
Min-temp	Calculate average temperature	
	Print average temperature	

The requirements of this example are similar to those in Example 3.1. Using pseudocode, a simple calculation and the sequence control structure the algorithm can be expressed as follows:

b Solution algorithm

```
Find-Average-Temperature
    Read Max-temp, Min-temp
    Avg-temp = (Max-temp + Min-temp) / 2
    Print Avg-temp
END
```

In this example the step 'Calculate average temperature' in the defining diagram has been expressed in the algorithm as an actual calculation to compute the average temperature.

A N–S diagram could have been used to express the solution algorithm to Example 3.2 as follows:

Find-Average-Temperature

Read Max-temp, Min-temp
Avg-temp = (Max-temp + Min-temp) / 2
Print Avg-temp

Example 3.3 Calculate coin denominations

A program is required to read in an amount of a purchase in pence, which is not to exceed one pound. The change from one pound is then to be calculated and printed as the most compact set of change (ie the fewest coins). It is assumed that the denominations available are 50p, 20p, 10p, 5p, 2p and 1p.

a Defining diagram

INPUT	*PROCESSING*	*OUTPUT*
Pence-amount	Read purchase amount Calculate change from £1.00 Calculate set of change Print set of change	Set-of-change

The three processing steps, 'Read purchase amount', 'Calculate change from £1.00' and 'Print set of change' are easy to express in an algorithm, using pseudocode. However, the step 'Calculate set of change' implies several tasks to be performed, as there are six different coin denominations to be determined. This step can be expressed more specifically by breaking it into a sequence of separate calculations to incorporate each denomination. First, calculate the number of 50p coins in the change, then the number of 20p coins, and so on. We can represent this breaking down process by expanding the processing component of the defining diagram as follows:

```
Read purchase amount
Calculate change from £1.00
Calculate set of change
   Compute number 50p coins
   Compute number 20p coins
   Compute number 10p coins
   Compute number 5p coins
   Compute number 2p coins
   Compute number 1p coins
Print set of change
```

This development from a general definition to a more detailed definition illustrates the first steps in the process of top-down design. The process will be described in more detail when hierarchy charts and modules are presented in Chapter 7.

At this stage, the processing steps still only describe the steps to be performed, in their correct order. To actually calculate the coin denominations, a series of divisions must be performed. Each division will yield both an integer part (to compute the number of whole coins) and a remainder (to be used in the next division). After the number of coins for each denomination has been calculated, the remaining change must also be determined.

In other words, the step 'Compute number of 50p coins' in the defining diagram will be expressed as two statements in the algorithm; one to compute the number of whole 50p coins, and another to calculate the remaining change. Meaningful names, such as '50p-coins' should be given to the variables within the algorithm for readability.

b The solution algorithm

```
Calculate-Set-of-Change
    Read Pence-amount
    Change = 100 - Pence-amount
    50p-coins = Change/50 (integer part)
    Change = Change - (50p-coins * 50)
    20p-coins = Change/20
    Change = Change - (20p-coins * 20)
    10p-coins = Change/10
    Change = Change - (10p-coins * 10)
    5p-coins = Change/5
    Change = Change - (5p-coins * 5)
    2p-coins = Change/2
    Change = Change - (2p-coins * 2)
    1p-coins = Change
    Print Set-of-change (ie Number of Fifty-pence-coins,
                            Twenty-pence-coins, etc)
END
```

It should be noted that this solution is not by any means the only solution, nor is it necessarily the best solution. The algorithm could be enhanced in several ways, by modularization, and by introducing some early exits, once the remaining change is found to be zero. These enhancements will be left for later chapters.

A N–S diagram could also have been used to express the solution algorithm to Example 3.3 as follows:

Calculate-Set-of-Change

Read Pence-amount
Change = 100 – Pence-amount
50p-coins = Change/50
Change = Change – (50p-coins * 50)
20p-coins = Change/20
Change = Change – (20p-coins * 20)
10p-coins = Change/10
Change = Change – (10p-coins * 10)
5p-coins = Change/5
Change = Change – (5p-coins * 5)
2p-coins = Change/2
Change = Change – (2p-coins * 2)
1p-coins = Change
Print Set-of-Change

3.3 Checking the solution algorithm

After a solution algorithm has been constructed, the algorithm must be tested for correctness. This is necessary, because most major logic errors occur during the development of the algorithm. If the algorithm contains errors, then these will be passed on to the program, and it is much easier to detect errors in pseudocode, than in the corresponding program code. Once programming begins, the programmer assumes that the logic of the algorithm is correct. Then, when errors are detected, the programmer's attention is focused on the individual lines of code to identify the problems rather than the initial logic expressed in the algorithm. It is often too difficult to step back and analyze the program as a whole. As a result, many frustrating hours can be wasted during testing, which could have been avoided, had the programmer stopped to spend just five minutes desk checking the solution algorithm.

Desk checking involves tracing through the logic of the algorithm with some chosen test data. That is, the programmer runs through the logic of the program exactly as a computer would, keeping track of all variable values on a sheet of paper. This *playing computer* not only helps to detect errors early, but also helps familiarize the programmer with the way the program runs. The closer the programmer is to the execution of the program, the easier it is to detect errors.

Steps in desk checking an algorithm

There are six simple steps to follow when desk checking an algorithm:

1 Choose simple input test cases which are valid. Two or three test cases are usually sufficient.
2 Establish what the expected result should be for each test case. This is one of the reasons for choosing simple test data in the first place — it is easier to determine what the total of 10, 20 and 30 is, rather than 3.75, 2.89 and 5.31!
3 Make a table of the relevant variable names within the algorithm on a piece of paper.
4 *Walk* the first test case through the algorithm keeping a step-by-step record of the contents of each variable in the table as the data passes through the logic.
5 Repeat the *walkthrough* process using the other test data cases, until the algorithm has reached its logical end.
6 Check that the *expected result* established in Step 2 matches the *actual result* developed in Step 5.
7 It should be understood that by desk checking an algorithm, a programmer is attempting to detect early errors. Desk checking will eliminate most errors, but it still cannot *prove* that the algorithm is one hundred percent correct!

Now let us desk check each of the algorithms developed in this chapter:

Example 3.1 Add three numbers

a Solution algorithm

```
Add-Three-Numbers
    Read Number1, Number2, Number3
    Total = Number1 + Number2 + Number3
    Print Total
END
```

b Desk checking

(i) Choose two sets of input test data, and establish the expected result.

(i) Input Data:

	First Data Set	Second Data Set
Number1	10	40
Number2	20	41
Number3	30	42

(ii) Expected Result:

Total	60	123

(ii) Set up a table of relevant variable names, and pass each test data set through the solution algorithm, statement by statement.

Statement		*Number1*	*Number2*	*Number3*	*Total*	*Print*
First Pass	Read	10	20	30		
	Total				60	
	Print					Yes
Second Pass	Read	40	41	42		
	Total				123	
	Print					Yes

(iii) Check that expected results (60 and 123) match the actual results (Total column in the table).

This desk check, which should take no more than five minutes to perform, indicates that the algorithm is correct. The programmer can now proceed to code his algorithm into a programming language.

Example 3.2 is very similar in operation to Example 3.1, so we will now desk check the solution algorithm to Example 3.3.

Example 3.3 Calculate coin denominations

a Solution algorithm

```
Calculate-Set-of-Change
   Read Pence-amount
   Change = 100 - Pence-amount
   50p-coins = Change/50
   Change = Change - (50p-coins * 50)
   20p-coins = Change/20
   Change = Change - (20p-coins * 20)
   10p-coins = Change/10
   Change = Change - (10p-coins * 10)
   5p-coins = Change/5
   Change = Change - (5p-coins * 5)
   2p-coins = Change/2
   Change = Change - (2p-coins * 2)
   1p-coins = Change
   Print Set-of-change
END
```

b Desk checking

(i) Choose 2 sets of valid input data and establish the expected result.

(i) Input Data:

	First Data Set	Second Data Set
Pence-Amount	75p	20p

(ii) Expected Result:

	First Data Set	Second Data Set
Expected change	25p	80p
Expected set of change	1 × 20p 1 × 5p	1 × 50p 1 × 20p 1 × 10p

(ii) Set up a table of variable names and pass each test data set through the solution algorithm, statement by statement.

Statement		Pence-amount	Change	50p-coins	20p-coins	10p-coins	5p-coins	2p-coins	1p-coins	Print
First Pass	Read	75p								
	Change		25p							
	50p-coins			0						
	Change		25p							
	20p-coins				1					
	Change		5p							
	10p-coins					0				
	Change		5p							
	5p-coins						1			
	Change		0							
	2p-coins							0		
	Change		0							
	1p-coins								0	
	Print									Yes
Second Pass	Read	20p								
	Change		80p							
	50p-coins			1						
	Change		30p							
	20p-coins				1					
	Change		10p							
	10p-coins					1				
	Change		0							
	5p-coins						0			
	Change		0							
	2p-coins							0		
	Change		0							
	1p-coins								0	
	Print									Yes

(iii) Check expected results match actual results

Yes, the expected result for each set of data matches the calculated result.

The desk checking of this example has illustrated a number of points. Firstly, algorithms containing a series of mathematical calculations must be checked thoroughly on paper before the commencement of program coding. Secondly, the algorithm could be improved, to ensure that no further testing of the coin denominations is performed once the change reaches zero. This improvement could easily be added to the algorithm in pseudocode, as will be illustrated in the next chapter.

3.4 Chapter summary

The first section of this chapter was devoted to methods of analyzing and defining a programming problem. A programmer must fully understand a problem before he or she can attempt to find a solution. The method suggested was an analysis of the actual words used in the specification to divide the problem into three separate components; input, output and processing. It was emphasized that the processing steps should list *what* tasks need to be performed, rather than *how* they are to be accomplished. Several examples were explored and the use of a defining diagram was established.

After the initial analysis of the problem, the programmer must attempt to find a solution, and express this solution as an algorithm. The second section of this chapter was devoted to the establishment of a solution algorithm. For this, a programmer must use correct pseudocode statements, the three basic control structures and the defining diagram which had previously been established. Only algorithms using the sequence control structure were used. Each solution was also expressed as a Nassi–Schneiderman diagram.

The third section of this chapter was concerned with the checking of the algorithm for correctness. A method of *playing computer* by tracing through the algorithm step by step was introduced, with examples to previous problems given. Desk checking will be further enhanced in the following chapters.

3.5 Programming problems

The following problems require the student to complete these tasks:

- define the problem by constructing a defining diagram,
- create a solution algorithm using pseudocode, or a Nassi–Schneiderman diagram, and
- desk check the solution algorithm using two valid test cases.

1 A program is required which will read in a tax rate as a percentage and the prices of five items. The program is to calculate the total price before tax of the items and then the tax payable on those items. The tax payable is computed by applying the tax rate percentage to the total price. Both values are to be printed as output.

2 A program is required to read in one customer's account balance at the beginning of a month, a total of all withdrawals for the month, and a total of all deposits made during the month. A tax charge of 1% is applied to all transactions made during the month. The program is to calculate the account balance at the end of the month by subtracting the total withdrawals, adding the total deposits and subtracting the tax from the account balance at the beginning of the month. After calculation the end of the month account balance is to be printed.

3 A program is required which will read in the values from an employee's time sheet, and calculate and print the weekly pay owing to that employee. The values read in are the total number of regular hours worked, the total overtime hours, and the hourly wage rate. Payment for regular hours worked is to be computed as rate times hours; payment for overtime hours is to be computed at time and a half. Weekly pay is calculated as payment for regular hours worked, plus payment for overtime hours worked.

CHAPTER 4

SELECTION CONTROL STRUCTURES

Objectives

- To elaborate on the uses of simple selection, multiple selection and nested selection in algorithms
- To introduce the *case* construct in pseudocode
- To develop algorithms using variations of the selection control structure

Outline

4.1 The selection control structure

The selection control structure was introduced in Chapter 2, as the second construct in the Structure Theorem. This structure represents the decision making abilities of the computer. That is, a programmer would use the selection control structure in pseudocode to illustrate a choice between two or more actions, depending on whether a certain condition is true or false. There are a number of variations of the selection structure, and these will be considered in detail.

1 Simple selection (Simple IF statement)

Simple selection occurs when a choice is made between two alternative paths, depending on the result of a condition being true or false. The structure is represented in pseudocode using the keywords IF, THEN, ELSE and ENDIF. For example:

```
IF accountbalance < £300 THEN
   service-charge = £5.00
ELSE
   service-charge = £2.00
ENDIF
```

Only one of the THEN or ELSE paths will be followed, depending on the result of the condition in the IF clause.

2 Simple selection with null false branch (null ELSE statement)

The null ELSE structure is a variation of the simple IF structure. It is used when a task is performed only when a particular condition is true. If the condition is false, then no processing will take place, and the IF statement will be bypassed. For example:

```
IF student-attendance = parttime THEN
   add 1 to parttime-count
ENDIF
```

In this case, the parttime-count field will only be altered if the student's attendance pattern is part time.

3 Combined selection (Combined IF statement)

A combined IF statement is one which contains multiple conditions, each connected with the logical operators AND, or OR. If the conditions are combined with the connector AND, then both conditions must be true for the combined condition to be true. For example:

```
IF student-attendance = parttime
AND student-sex = female THEN
   add 1 to fem-parttime-count
ENDIF
```

In this case, each student record will undergo two tests. Only those students who are female, and whose attendance pattern is part time will be selected, and the variable fem-parttime-count will be incremented. If either condition is found to be false, then the counter will remain unchanged.

If the connector OR is used to combine any two conditions, then only one of the conditions needs to be true for the combined condition to be considered true. If neither condition is true, then the combined condition is considered false. For example, if we change the AND in the above example to OR then the outcome from the processing of the IF statement will change dramatically.

```
IF student-attendance = parttime
OR student-sex = female THEN
   add 1 to fem-parttime-count
ENDIF
```

In the above example, if either one, or both conditions, is found to be true then the combined condition will be considered true. That is the counter will be incremented:

1 if the student is part time, regardless of sex; and
2 if the student is female, regardless of attendance pattern.

Only those students who are not female, and not part time will be ignored. So, fem-parttime-count will contain the total count of female part time students, male part time students, and female full time students. As a result fem-parttime-count is no longer a meaningful name for this variable. Programmers must fully understand the processing which takes place when combining conditions with the AND or OR logical operators.

More than two conditions can be linked together with the AND operator or the OR operator. However, if both an AND and an OR are used in the one IF statement, then brackets must be used to avoid ambiguity. Look at the following example:

```
IF record-code = '23'
OR update-code = delete
AND account-balance = zero THEN
   delete customer record
ENDIF
```

The logic of this statement is confusing. It is uncertain whether the first two conditions should be grouped together and operated on first, or the second two conditions should be grouped together and operated on first. Pseudocode algorithms should never be ambiguous. There are no precedence rules for logical operators in pseudocode, so brackets must be used to explicitly state the intended order of processing as follows:

```
IF (record-code = '23'
OR update-code = delete)
AND account-balance = zero THEN
   delete customer record
ENDIF
```

4 Nested selection (Nested IF statement)

Nested selection occurs when the word IF appears more than once within an IF statement. Nested IF statements can be classified as linear or non-linear.

a Linear nested IF statements

The linear nested IF statement is used when a field is being tested for various values, with a different action to be taken for each value.

This form of nested IF is called linear because each ELSE immediately follows the IF condition to which it corresponds. Comparisons are made until a true condition is encountered, and the specified action or actions are executed until the next ELSE statement is reached. Linear nested IF statements should be indented for readability, with each IF, ELSE and corresponding ENDIF aligned.

For example:

```
IF record-code = 'A' THEN
   increment counterA
ELSE
   IF record-code = 'B' THEN
      increment counterB
   ELSE
      IF record-code = 'C' THEN
         increment counterC
      ELSE
```

```
            increment error-counter
        ENDIF
    ENDIF
ENDIF
```

Note that there are an equal number of IF, ELSE and ENDIF statements, and that the correct indentation makes it easy to read and understand.

b Non-linear nested IF statements

A non-linear nested IF occurs when a number of different conditions need to be satisfied before a particular action can occur. It is termed non-linear because the ELSE statement may be separated from the IF statement with which it is paired. Indentation is once again important when expressing this form of selection in pseudocode. Each ELSE statement should be aligned with the IF condition to which it corresponds.

For instance:

```
IF student-attendance = parttime THEN
    IF student-sex = female THEN
        IF student-age > 21 THEN
            add 1 to mature-fem-pt-students
        ELSE
            add 1 to young-fem-pt-students
        ENDIF
    ELSE
        add 1 to male-pt-students
    ENDIF
ELSE
    add 1 to fulltime-students
ENDIF
```

Note that there are an equal number of IF conditions as ELSE and ENDIF statements. Using correct indentation helps to see which pair of IF and ELSE statements match. However, the above example may contain logic errors which could be difficult to correct. As a result, non-linear nested IF statements should be used sparingly in pseudocode. If possible, replace a series of non-linear nested IF statements with a combined IF statement.

This replacement is possible in pseudocode because two consecutive IF statements act like a combined IF statement which uses the AND operator. For instance, the following non-linear nested IF statement:

```
IF student-attendance = parttime THEN
   IF student-age > 21 THEN
      increment mature-pt-student
   ENDIF
ENDIF
```

can be written as a combined IF statement;

```
IF student-attendance = parttime
AND student-age > 21 THEN
   increment mature-pt-student
ENDIF
```

The same outcome will occur for both pseudocode expressions, however the format of the latter is preferred, if the logic allows it, simply because it is easier to understand.

5 Nassi–Schneiderman diagrams and the selection control structure

Each variation of the selection structure developed in pseudocode can similarly be represented using a Nassi–Schneiderman diagram.

1 Simple IF statement

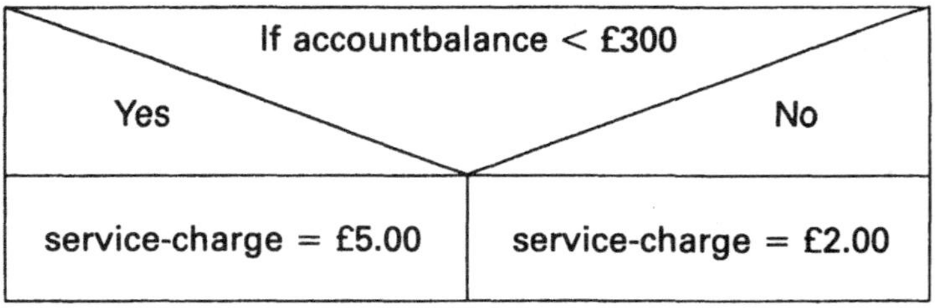

2 Null ELSE statement

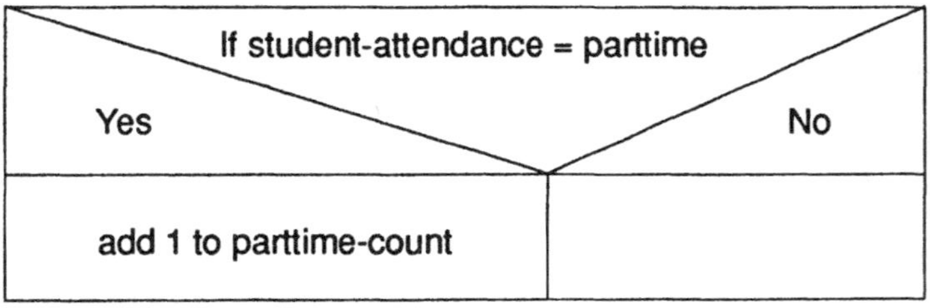

3 Combined IF statement

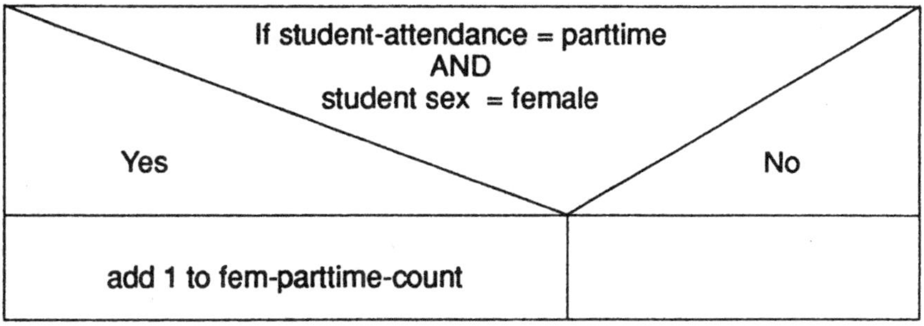

4 Nested IF statement

a Linear nested IF statement

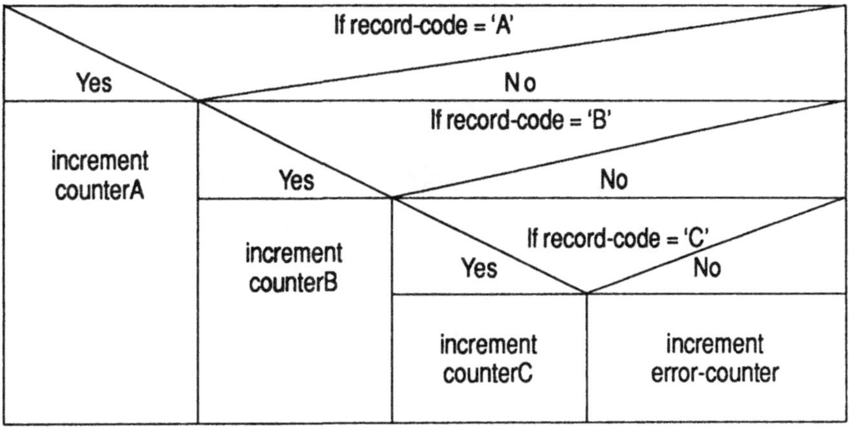

b Non-linear nested IF statement

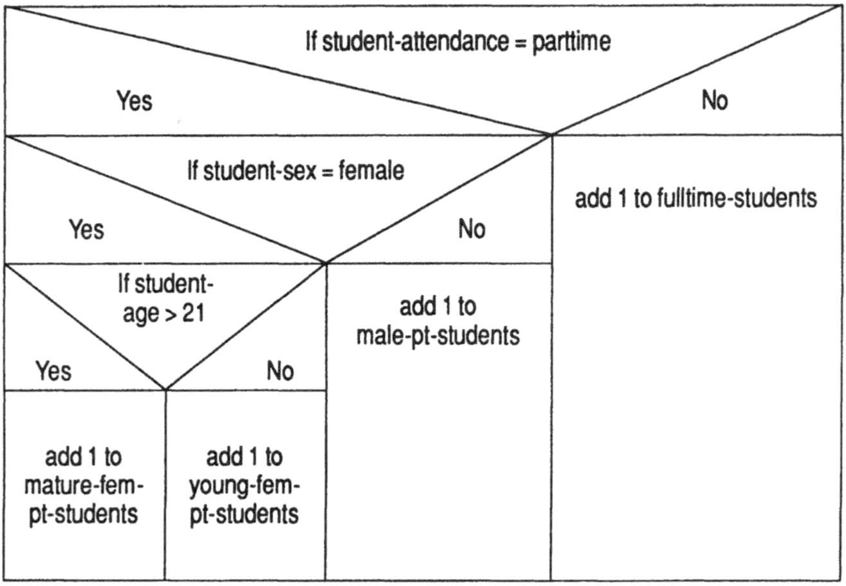

4.2 Programming examples using selection

Let us look at some programming examples which use the selection control structure. In each example, the problem will be defined, a solution algorithm will be developed and the algorithm will be manually tested. For ease in defining the problem, the processing verbs in each example have been underlined. Note that in the next example we are ignoring VAT.

Example 4.1 Process customer record

A programmer is required to read a customer's name, a purchase amount and a discount code. The discount code has been validated and will be one of the following:

0 no discount (0%)
1 3% discount
2 5% discount
3 7% discount

The program is required to compute the discount and total amount due and print the customer's name, purchase amount, discount and total amount due.

a Defining diagram

INPUT	*PROCESSING*	*OUTPUT*
Cust-name	Read customer details	Cust-name
Purch-amt	Compute Discount Amount	Purch-amt
Disc-code	Compute Total Amount	Discount
	Print customer details	Total-Amt

b Solution algorithm

The solution algorithm requires a linear nested IF to calculate the discount.

```
Process-Customer-Record
   Read Cust-name, Purch-amt, Disc-code
   IF Disc-code = 0 THEN
      Discount = 0
   ELSE
      IF Disc-code = 1 THEN
         Discount = Purch-amt * 0.03
      ELSE
         IF Disc-code = 2 THEN
            Discount = Purch-amt * 0.05
         ELSE
            Discount = Purch-amt * 0.07
         ENDIF
      ENDIF
   ENDIF
   Total-Amt = Purch-amt – Discount
   Print Cust-name, Purch-amt, Discount, Total-Amt
END
```

The solution algorithm can also be represented by a N–S diagram:

Process-Customer-Record

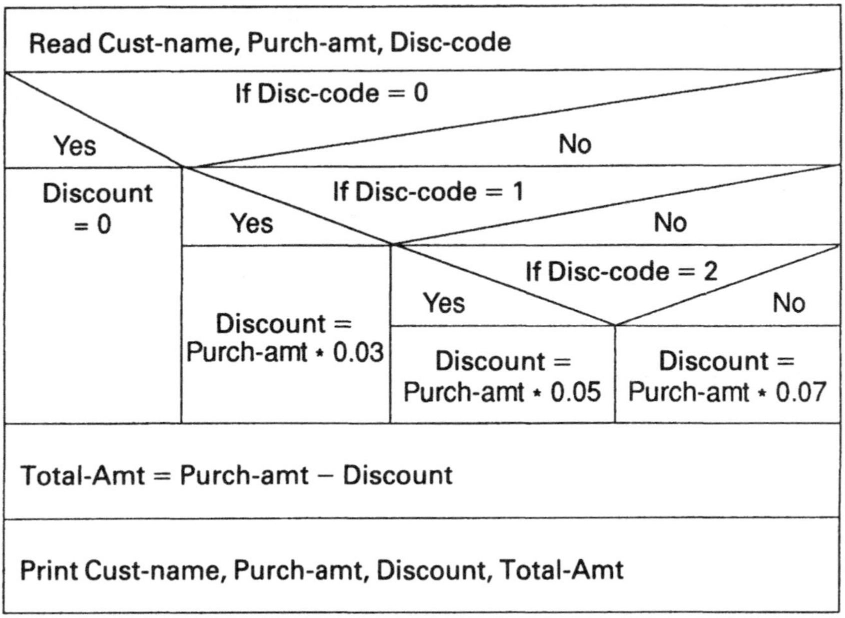

c Desk checking

Two sets of valid input data for purchase amount and discount code will be used to check the algorithm.

(i) Input Data:

	First Data Set	Second Data Set
Purch-amt	10.00	20.00
Disc-code	0	2

(ii) Expected Result:

	First Data Set	Second Data Set
Discount	0	1.00
Total-Amt	10.00	19.00

Note that when desk checking the logic, the whole linear nested IF statement (13 lines of pseudocode) is counted as a single pseudocode statement.

(iii) Desk Check Table:

Statement		Purch-amt	Disc-code	Discount	Total-Amt	Print
	Read	10.00	0			
First	IF			0		
Pass	Total				10.00	
	Print					Yes
Second	Read	20.00	2			
Pass	IF			1.00		
	Total				19.00	
	Print					Yes

As the expected result for the two test cases matches the calculated result, the algorithm is correct.

Example 4.2 Calculate employee's pay

A program is required by a company to read an employee's number, pay rate and the number of hours worked in a week. The program is then to compute the employee's weekly pay and print it along with the input data. According to the company's rules, no employee may be paid for more than 60 hours per week, and the maximum hourly rate is £25.00 per hour. If more than 35 hours are worked, then payment for the overtime hours worked is calculated at time and a half. If the hours worked field or the hourly rate field is out of range, then the input data and an appropriate message is to be printed, and the employee's weekly pay is not to be calculated.

a Defining diagram

INPUT	*PROCESSING*	*OUTPUT*
Emp-no	Read employee details	Emp-no
Pay-rate	Validate input fields	Pay-rate
Hrs-worked	Compute emp-weekly-pay	Hrs-worked
	Print employee details	Emp-weekly-pay
	Print appropriate message	Error-message

b Solution algorithm

The solution to this problem will require a series of simple IF and nested IF statements. Firstly, the variables 'Pay-rate' and 'Hrs- worked' must be validated, and if either is found to be out of range then an appropriate message should be placed into a variable called 'Error-message'.

The employee's weekly pay is only to be calculated if the variables 'Pay-rate' and 'Hrs-worked' are valid, so another variable 'All-fields-valid' will be used to indicate to the program whether or not the weekly pay is to be calculated.

The variable 'All-fields-valid' acts as an internal *switch* or *flag* to the program. It will initially be set to *true,* and will be assigned the value *false* if one of the fields is found to be invalid. The employee's weekly pay will only be calculated if 'All-fields-valid' is *true.*

```
Compute-Employee-Pay
   Set All-fields-valid to true
   Set Error-message to blank
   Read Emp-no, Pay-rate, Hrs-worked
   IF Pay-rate > £25.00 THEN
      Error-message = 'Pay rate exceeds £25.00'
      All-fields-valid = false
   ELSE
      IF Hrs-worked > 60 THEN
         Error-message = 'Hours worked exceeds limit of 60'
         All-fields-valid = false
      ENDIF
   ENDIF
   IF All-fields-valid = false THEN
      Print Emp-no, Pay-rate, Hrs-worked, Error-message
   ELSE
      IF Hrs-worked < = 35 THEN
         Emp-weekly-pay = Pay-rate * Hrs-worked
         Print Emp-no, Pay-rate, Hrs-worked, Emp-weekly-pay
      ELSE
         Overtime-hrs = Hrs-worked – 35
         Overtime-pay = Overtime-hrs * Pay-rate * 1.5
         Emp-weekly-pay = (Pay-rate * 35) + Overtime-pay
         Print Emp-no, Pay-rate, Hrs-worked, Emp-weekly-pay
      ENDIF
   ENDIF
END
```

As can been seen in the above solution, there are two separate functions to be performed in this algorithm; the validation of the input data; and the calculation and printing of the Employee's weekly pay.

These two tasks could have been separated into modules, before the algorithm was developed in pseudocode. Breaking a problem into modules will be discussed in Chapter 7.

The solution algorithm can also be represented by a N–S diagram:

Compute-Employee-Pay

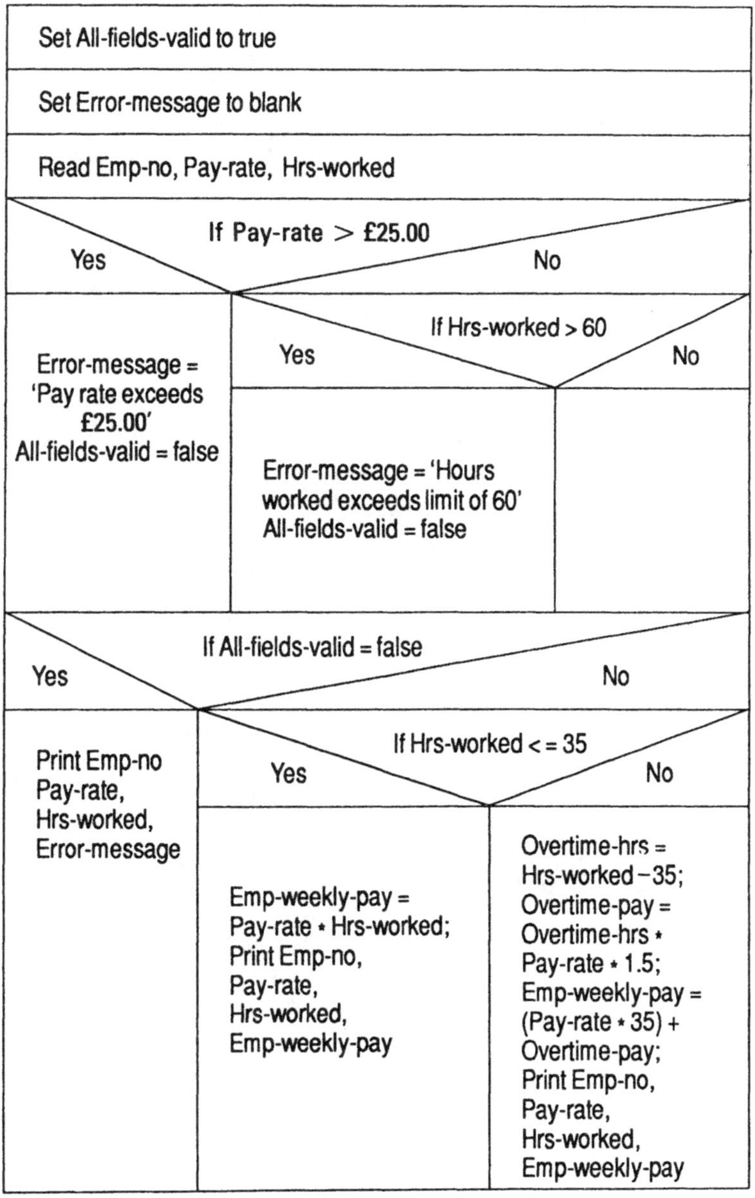

c Desk checking

(i) Input Data:

	First Data Set	Second Data Set
Pay-rate	£10	£40
Hrs-worked	40	35

(ii) Expected Result:

	First Data Set	Second Data Set
Pay-rate	£10	£40
Hrs-worked	40	35
Emp-weekly-pay	£425	not calculated
Error-message	blank	'Pay rate exceeds £25.00'

(iii) Desk Check Table:

Statement		All-fields-valid	Error-Message	Pay-rate	Hrs-worked	Ovt-Hrs	Ovt-Pay	Emp-weekly-Pay
First Pass	Set All-fields-valid	true						
	Set-Error-Message		blank					
	Read			£10	40			
	If Pay-rate							
	If All-fields-valid					5	£75	425
				Print	Print			Print
Second Pass	Set All-fields-valid	true						
	Set-Error-Message		blank					
	Read			£40	35			
	If Pay-rate	false	'pay-rate exceeds £25.00'					
	If All-fields-valid		Print	Print	Print			

Example 4.3 Calculate coin denominations

Let us now look at the Calculate coin denominations example, introduced in Chapter 3. By using the selection control structure, the solution algorithm can be improved, so that, once there is no change left, no further calculations will be performed. The improved algorithm might look like this:

```
Calculate-Set-Of-Change
    Read Pence-amount
    Change = 100 – Pence-amount
    IF Change not zero THEN
        50p-coins = Change/50
        Change = Change – (50p-coins * 50)
    ENDIF
    IF Change not zero THEN
        20p-coins = Change/20
        Change = Change – (20p-coins * 20)
    ENDIF
    IF Change not zero THEN
        10p-coins = Change/10
        Change = Change – (10p-coins * 10)
    ENDIF
    IF Change not zero THEN
        5p-coins = Change/5
        Change = Change – (5p-coins * 5)
    ENDIF
    IF Change not zero THEN
        2p-coins = Change/2
        Change = Change – (2p-coins * 2)
    ENDIF
    One-pence coins = Change
    Print Set-of-change
END
```

This algorithm has been improved to become more efficient, and more sophisticated. However there are still further improvements which could be effected. At the moment the algorithm looks cumbersome and repetitive. It could be altered to incorporate the use of modules to perform some of the calculations, and improve readability. Modularization will be discussed in Chapter 7.

4.3 The *case* structure

The *case* control structure in pseudocode is another way of expressing a linear nested IF statement. It is used in pseudocode for two reasons. Firstly, it can be directly translated into many high level languages, and secondly, it makes the pseudocode easier to write and understand. Nested IFs often look cumbersome in pseudocode and are dependent on correct structure and indentation for readability. Let us look at an example used earlier in this chapter:

```
IF record-code = 'A' THEN
   increment counterA
ELSE
   IF record-code = 'B' THEN
      increment counterB
   ELSE
      IF record-code = 'C' THEN
         increment counterC
      ELSE
         increment error-counter
      ENDIF
   ENDIF
ENDIF
```

This linear nested IF structure can be replaced with a *case* control structure. *Case* is not really an additional control structure. It simply generalizes the basic selection control structure and extends it from a choice between two values, to a choice from multiple values. In one *case* structure, several alternative logical paths can be represented. In pseudocode, the keywords CASE OF and ENDCASE serve to identify the structure, with the multiple values indented, as follows:

```
CASE OF single variable
   value1 : statement block1
   value2 : statement block2

   valuen : statement blockn
   value other : statement block other
ENDCASE
```

The path followed in the *case* structure depends on the value of the variable specified in the CASE OF clause. If the variable contains 'value1' then statement block1 is executed; if it contains 'value2', then statement block2 is executed, and so on. The 'value other' is included in the event that the variable contains none of the listed values. We can now rewrite the linear nested IF statement with a *case* statement, as follows:

```
CASE OF record-code
      'A' :  increment counterA
      'B' :  increment counterB
      'C' :  increment counterC
   other :  increment error-counter
ENDCASE
```

In both forms of pseudocode, the processing logic is exactly the same. However, the *case* solution is much more readable.

The *case* control structure can also be represented by a N–S diagram:

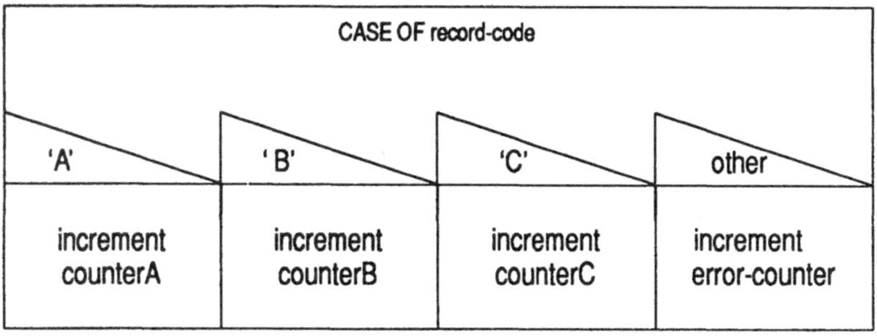

Example 4.4 Calculate sales commission

A transaction record on a Sales Commission File contains the retail price of an item sold, a transaction code which indicates the sales commission category to which an item can belong, and the employee number of the person who sold the item. The transaction code can contain the values S, M or L which indicate that the percentage commission will be 5%, 7% or 10% respectively. Construct an algorithm which will read a record on the file, calculate the commission owing for that record, and print the retail price, commission and employee number.

a Defining diagram

INPUT	*PROCESSING*	*OUTPUT*
Retail-price	Read transaction record	Retail-price
Transaction-code	Calculate commission	Commission
Emp-no	Print sales details	Emp-no

b Solution algorithm

It is assumed that the only valid transaction codes are S, M and L, and that any other code will render a zero commission.

```
Calculate-sales-commission
    Read Retail-price, Transaction-code, Emp-no
    CASE OF Transaction-code
        S     : Commission = Retail-price * 0.05
        M     : Commission = Retail-price * 0.07
        L     : Commission = Retail-price * 0.1
        other : Commission = zero
    ENDCASE
    Print Retail-price, Commission, Emp-no.
END
```

The solution algorithm can also be represented by a N–S diagram:

Calculate-sales-commission

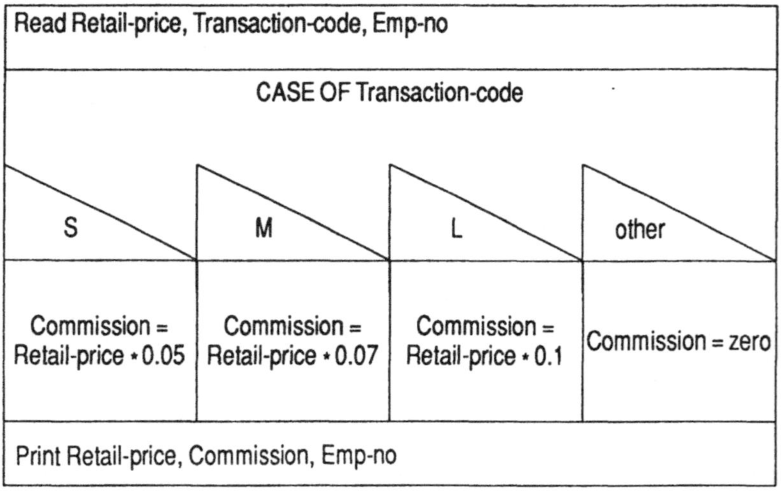

c Desk checking

Two sets of input data for Retail-price and Transaction-code will be used to check the algorithm. Note that the *case* structure serves as a single pseudocode statement.

(i) Input Data:

	First Data Set	Second Data Set
Retail-price	£100.00	£100.00
Transaction-code	S	K (invalid)

(ii) Expected Result:

	First Data Set	Second Data Set
Retail-price	£100.00	£100.00
Transaction-code	S	K (invalid)
Commission	£5.00	zero

(iii) Desk Check Table:

Statement		Retail-Price	Transaction-code	Commission
First	Read	100.00	S	
Pass	CASE			5.00
	Print	Print		Print
Second	Read	100.00	K	
Pass	CASE			zero
	Print	Print		Print

As the expected result matches the actual result the algorithm is shown to be correct.

4.4 Chapter summary

This chapter covered the selection control structure in detail. Descriptions and pseudocode examples were given for simple selection, null ELSE, combined IF and nested IF statements. Several solution algorithms which used the selection structure were developed.

The *case* structure was introduced as a means of expressing a linear nested IF statement in a simpler and more concise form. *Case* is available in many high level languages, and so is a useful construct to write in pseudocode.

4.5 Programming problems

Construct a solution algorithm for the following programming problems. Your solution should contain:

- a defining diagram
- a pseudocode algorithm, or Nassi–Schneiderman diagram, and
- a desk check of the algorithm.

1 A glass return company requires a program which will calculate the amount of credit due to a customer who returns a case, or cases of empty bottles. (One case contains 10 bottles.) Input to the program is a record, containing the customer's name and a number. This number contains the number of full or partly full cases of empty bottles, which the customer has returned (eg 8.5 indicates 8 full cases and one half-full case). If a case returned by a customer is more than half full, it is to be counted as full. If 8 or more cases are returned, the customer is to receive £4.00 per case, otherwise the customer receives £3.50 per case. The program is to print the customer's name, the number of cases returned, the number of full cases credited and the credit amount due.

2 A program is to be written which reads a four digit integer which represents the time of day in military time, converts it to civilian time and prints the result. Military time is expressed as HHMM, using a 24 hour clock (eg 1230 or 2245). Civilian time is to be expressed as HH:MM followed by either 'AM' or 'PM' (eg 12:30 AM or 10:45 PM). Before conversion, the input time should be validated to ensure it falls within an acceptable range (eg Military time must be >= 0001 and <= 2400).

3 A home mortgage authority requires a deposit on a home loan according to the following schedule:

£ Loan Amount	Deposit
Less than 25 000	5% of loan value
25 000 – 49 999	£1 250 + 10% of loan over £25 000
50 000 – 100 000	£5 000 + 25% of loan over £50 000

Loans in excess of £100 000 are not allowed. Design a program which will read a loan amount and compute and print the required deposit.

4 Design a program which will read two numbers and an integer code. The value of the code should be 1, 2, 3 or 4. If the value of the code is 1 then compute the sum of the two numbers. If the code is 2, then compute the difference (first minus second). If the code is 3, compute the product of the two numbers. If the code is 4, and the second number is not zero, then compute the quotient (first divided by second). The program is to print the two numbers, the integer code and the computed result.

CHAPTER 5

REPETITION CONTROL STRUCTURES

Objectives

- To develop algorithms which use the DOWHILE and REPEAT..UNTIL control structures
- To introduce a pseudocode structure for counted repetition loops
- To develop algorithms using variations of the repetition construct

Outline

5.1 Repetition using the DOWHILE structure

The solution algorithms developed so far have one characteristic in common – they show the program logic required to process just one set of input values. However, most programs require the same logic to be repeated for several sets of data. The most efficient way to deal with this situation is to establish a looping structure in the algorithm. This will cause the processing logic to be repeated a number of times.

In Chapter 2, the DOWHILE construct was introduced as the pseudocode representation of a repetitive loop. Its format is:

```
DOWHILE condition p is true
   statement block
ENDDO
```

As the DOWHILE loop is a leading decision loop, the following processing takes place:

a The logical condition p is tested
b If condition p is found to be true, then the statements within the statement block will be executed once. Control will then return to the retesting of the condition p (step a).
c If condition p is found to be false, then control will pass to the next statement after ENDDO and no further processing will take place.

As a result, the DOWHILE structure will continue to repeat a group of statements WHILE a condition remains true. As soon as the condition becomes false, the construct is exited.

There are two important considerations about which a programmer must be aware before designing a DOWHILE loop. Firstly, the testing of the condition is at the beginning of the loop. This means that the programmer may need to perform some initial processing to adequately *set-up* the condition before it can be tested. Secondly, the only way to terminate the loop is to render the DOWHILE condition false. This means that the programmer must set up some process within the statement block which will eventually change the condition so that the condition becomes false. Failure to do this results in an endless loop.

Example 5.1 Fahrenheit – Celsius conversion

A temperature file consists of fifteen records, each containing a temperature in degrees fahrenheit. A program is to be written which will read and print both temperatures in two columns on a report. Column headings which read 'Degrees F' and 'Degrees C' are to be printed at the top of the page.

a Defining diagram

INPUT	*PROCESSING*	*OUTPUT*
15 records	Print column headings	Headings
F-temp	For each record	F-temp
	Read F-temp	C-temp
	Convert F-temp to C-temp	
	Print F-temp, C-temp	

Note that the defining diagram still only lists *what* needs to be done. Having defined the input, output and processing, the programmer should now be ready to outline a solution to the problem. This can be done by writing down the control structures needed and any extra variables which are to be used in the solution algorithm. In this example, the programmer will need:

— a DOWHILE structure to repeat the necessary processing, and
— a counter, initialised at zero, which will control the fifteen repetitions. This counter, called record-counter, will contain the number of records read and processed.

The programmer should now write down the solution algorithm.

b Solution algorithm

```
Fahrenheit–Celsius conversion
    Print 'Degrees F' and 'Degrees C'
    Set record-counter to zero
    DOWHILE record-counter < 15
        Read F-temp
        Compute C-temp = (F-temp – 32) * 5/9
        Print F-temp, C-temp
        Add 1 to record-counter
    ENDDO
END
```

Note that the 'record-counter' variable is initialized before the loop, tested in the DOWHILE condition at the top of the loop, and incremented within the body of the loop. It is essential that the variable which controls the loop is acted upon in these three places. Notice, also, that the statement which alters the value of the record–counter in the loop, is the last statement in the statement block. That is, immediately after incrementing the record-counter, its value will be tested when control returns to the DOWHILE condition at the top of the loop.

The solution algorithm can also be represented by a N–S diagram:

Fahrenheit–Celsius conversion

Print 'Degrees F' and 'Degrees C'
Set record-counter to zero
DOWHILE record-counter < 15

Read F-temp
    Compute C-temp = (F-temp – 32) * 5/9
    Print F-temp, C-temp
    Add 1 to record-counter

c Desk checking

Although the program will require 15 records to process properly, it is still only necessary to check the algorithm at this stage with two valid sets of data

(i) Input Data:

	First Data Set	Second Data Set
F-temp	32	50

(ii) Expected Result:

Headings	Degrees F	Degrees C
Values	32	0
	50	10

(iii) Desk Check Table:

Statement	Print Heading	Record Counter	DOWHILE true?	F-temp	C-temp	Print Value
Print Headings	Yes					
Set record-counter		0				
DOWHILE condition			Yes			
Read F-temp				32		
Compute C-temp					0	
Print F-temp, C-temp						Yes
Inc. record-counter		1				
DOWHILE condition			Yes			
Read F-temp				50		
Compute C-temp					10	
Print F-temp, C-temp						Yes
Inc. record-counter		2				

The desk checking of this algorithm shows the exact processing of a DOWHILE loop. There is some initial processing (first two statements) which will only be executed once. Then the DOWHILE condition is tested, and found to be true. The body of the loop is then executed before returning to the testing of the DOWHILE condition. Processing will continue to repeat until the DOWHILE condition becomes false, ie the record counter is equal to 15.

Although only two test cases were used to desk check the algorithm, the programmer can see that, given more test cases, the record counter will eventually reach 15, and so the looping will cease.

Let us now look at a problem where an unknown number of records are to be processed. In this situation, the programmer cannot use a counter to control the loop, so another method is required. Often this takes the form of a trailer record, or *sentinel*. This sentinel is a special record placed at the end of the valid data, to signify the end of that data. It must contain a value which is clearly distinguishable from the other data to be processed. It is referred to as a sentinel, as it acts as an indication that no more data follows.

Example 5.2 Print examination scores

A program is required to read and print a series of names and exam scores for students enrolled in a mathematics course. The class average is to be computed and printed at the end of the report. Scores can range from 0 to 100. The last record contains a blank name and a score of 999 and is not to be included in the calculations.

a Defining diagram

INPUT	*PROCESSING*	*OUTPUT*
Student-records containing	For each record:	Student-report containing
Name	Read student record	Names
Exam-score	Print student record	Exam-scores
Record-999	Compute Average-score	Average-score
	Print Average-score	

The programmer will need to consider the following requirements when establishing a solution algorithm:

— a DOWHILE structure to control the reading of exam scores, until it reaches a score of 999.
— an accumulator for the total scores, viz Total-score.
— an accumulator for the total students, viz Total-students.

b Solution algorithm

```
Print-examination-scores
    Set Total-score to zero
    Set Total-students to zero
    Read Name, Exam-score
    DOWHILE Exam-score NOT = 999
        Add 1 to Total-students
        Print Name, Exam-score
        Add Exam-score to Total-score
        Read Name, Exam-score
    ENDDO
    Average-score = Total-score/Total-students
    Print Average-score
END
```

This solution algorithm is a typical example of the basic algorithm design required for processing sequential files of data. There is an unknown number of records, so the condition which controls the exam score processing is the testing for the trailer record (Record-999). It is this test which appears in the DOWHILE clause (DOWHILE Exam-score NOT = 999).

However, this test cannot be made until at least one exam score has been read. Hence, the initial processing, which *sets up* the condition, is a read statement immediately before the DOWHILE clause (Read Name, Exam-score). This is known as a *priming read* and its use is extremely important when processing sequential files.

The algorithm will require another *Read* statement, within the body of the loop. Its position is also important. The trailer record must not be included in the calculation of average score, so each time an exam score is read, it must be tested for a 999 value, before further processing can take place. For this reason the *Read* statement is placed at the end of the loop, immediately before ENDDO, so that its value can be tested when control returns to the DOWHILE condition. As soon as the trailer record has been read, control will exit from the loop to the next statement after ENDDO — the calculation of Average-score.

This priming read before the DOWHILE condition and subsequent read within the loop, immediately before the ENDDO statement, forms the basic framework for DOWHILE repetitions in pseudocode. In general, all algorithms using a DOWHILE construct to process a sequential file should have the same basic pattern, as follows:

```
Process-Sequential-file
   Do Initial processing
   Read first record
   DOWHILE more records exist
      Process this record
      Read next record
   ENDDO
   Do Final Processing
END
```

The solution algorithm to the Print examination scores example (Example 5.2) can also be represented by a N–S diagram:

```
Print-examination-scores
+------------------------------------------------------------+
| Set Total-score to zero                                    |
+------------------------------------------------------------+
| Set Total-students to zero                                 |
+------------------------------------------------------------+
| Read Name, Exam-score                                      |
+------------------------------------------------------------+
| DOWHILE Exam-score NOT = 999                               |
|                 +------------------------------------------+
|                 | Add 1 to Total-students                  |
|                 | Print Name, Exam-score                   |
|                 | Add Exam-score to Total-score            |
|                 | Read Name, Exam-score                    |
+-----------------+------------------------------------------+
| Average-score = Total-score/Total-students                 |
+------------------------------------------------------------+
| Print Average-score                                        |
+------------------------------------------------------------+
```

c Desk checking

Two valid records and a trailer record should be sufficient to desk check this algorithm.

(i) Input data:

	First Record	Second Record	Third Record
Score	50	100	999

(ii) Expected output:

First record — score 50
Second record — score 100
Average score — 75

(iii) Desk Check Table:

Statement	Total-Score	Total-Students	Exam-Score	DOWHILE true?	Print	Average-Score
Init Total-score	0					
Init Total-students		0				
Read record			50			
DOWHILE cond.				yes		
Add to Total-Students		1				
Print record					yes	
Add to Total-score	50					
Read record			100			
DOWHILE cond.				yes		
Add to Total-Students		2				
Print record					yes	
Add to Total-score	150					
Read record			999			
DOWHILE cond.				no		
Average-score						75
Print Average-Score					yes	

Example 5.3 Process student enrolments

A program is required which will read a file of student records, and select and print only those students enrolled in a course unit named Programming I. Each student record contains student number, name, address, postcode, sex and course unit number. The course unit number for Programming I is 18500. Three totals are to be printed at the end of the report: total females enrolled in the course; total males enrolled in the course, and total students enrolled in the course.

a Defining diagram

INPUT	*PROCESSING*	*OUTPUT*
Student-records containing	For each record	Selected student records
– student-no	Read student record	Total-Females -Enrolled
– name	Print student details	Total-Males -Enrolled
– address	Increment Total-Females -Enrolled	Total-Students -Enrolled
– postcode	Increment Total-Males -Enrolled	
– student-sex	Increment Total-Students -Enrolled	
– course-unit	Print Total-Females-Enrolled	
	Print Total Males-Enrolled	
	Print Total-Students-Enrolled	

The programmer will need to consider the following requirements, when establishing a solution algorithm:

—a DOWHILE structure to perform the repetition,
—an IF statement to select the required students, and
—accumulators for the three total fields.

It should be noted that there is no trailer record for this student file. In cases like this, the terms *more data, more records, records exist* or *not end of file (EOF)* can be used in the DOWHILE condition clause.

For example, DOWHILE more data, OR
DOWHILE more records, OR
DOWHILE records exist, OR
DOWHILE not EOF.
are all equivalent conditions.

By expressing the condition in this way, the programmer leaves it to the computer machinery to indicate to the program when there are no more records in the file. This occurs when an attempt is made to read a record, but no more records exist. A signal is sent to the program to indicate that there are no more records, and so the *DOWHILE more records* or *DOWHILE not EOF* clause is rendered false.

b Solution algorithm

```
Process-student-enrolments
   Set Total-Females-Enrolled to zero
   Set Total-Males-Enrolled to zero
   Set Total-Students-Enrolled to zero
   Read student record
   DOWHILE records exist
      IF course-unit = 18500 THEN
         print student details
         increment Total-Students-Enrolled
         IF student-sex = female THEN
            increment Total-Females-Enrolled
         ELSE
            increment Total-Males-Enrolled
         ENDIF
      ENDIF
      Read student record
   ENDDO
   Print Total-Females-Enrolled
   Print Total-Males-Enrolled
   Print Total-Students-Enrolled
END
```

This solution algorithm uses the same basic framework as the previous example. A non-linear nested IF statement was used to determine the required selection logic.

The solution algorithm can also be represented by a N–S diagram:

Process-student-enrolments

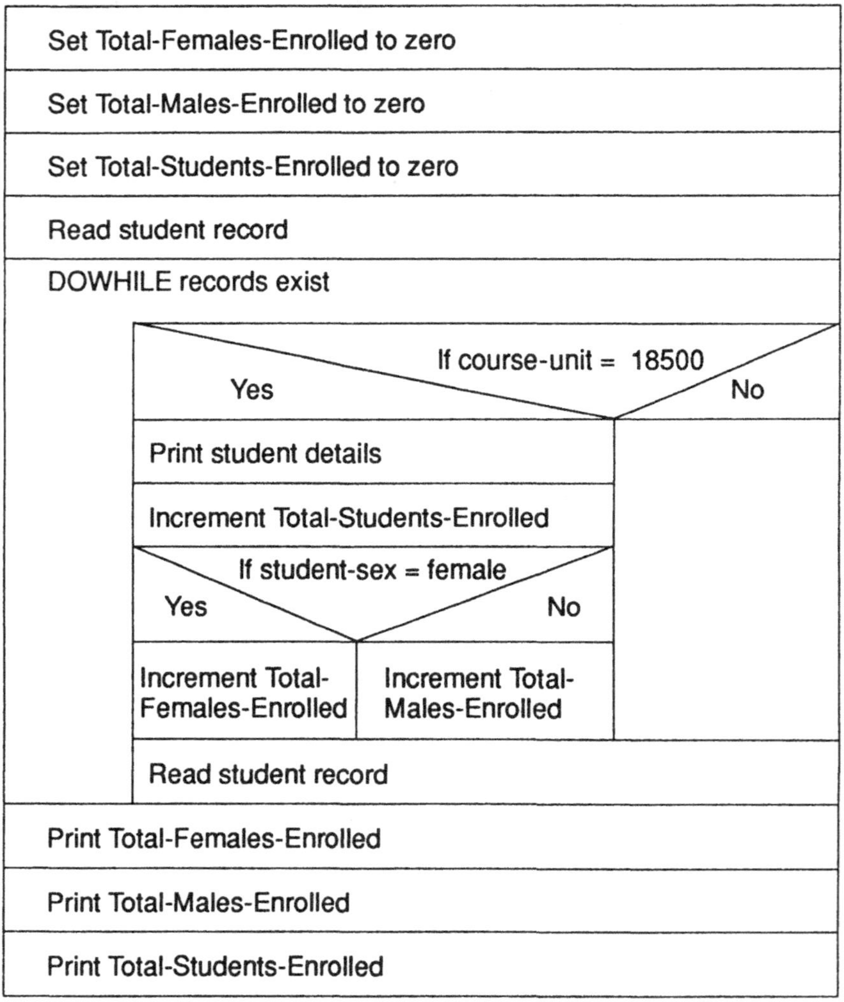

c Desk checking

Three valid records should be sufficient to desk check this algorithm.

(i) Input Data:

	First Record	Second Record	Third Record
course-unit	20000	18500	18500
student-sex	F	F	M

(ii) Expected Output:

Student Name, no, address,	F	(2nd student)
Student Name, no, address,	M	(3rd student)
Total Females Enrolled	1	
Total Males Enrolled	1	
Total Students Enrolled	2	

(iii) Desk Check Table:

The non linear nested IF statement in this example will be considered a single statement when desk checking the algorithm.

Statement	Total-Females-Enrolled	Total-Males-Enrolled	Total-Students-Enrolled	course-unit	student-sex	DOWHILE true?	Print
Init Total	0						
Init Total		0					
Init Total			0				
Read record				20000	F		
DOWHILE cond.						Yes	
IF statement							No
Read record				18500	F		
DOWHILE cond.						Yes	
IF statement	1		1				Yes
Read record				18500	M		
DOWHILE cond.						Yes	
IF statement		1	2				Yes
Read record				EOF			
DOWHILE cond.						No	
Print Total	Print						
Print Total		Print					
Print Total			Print				

5.2 Repetition using the REPEAT..UNTIL structure

The REPEAT..UNTIL structure is similar to the DOWHILE structure, in that a group of statements are repeated, in accordance with a specified condition. However, where the DOWHILE structure tests the condition at the beginning of the loop, a REPEAT..UNTIL structure tests the condition at the end of the loop. This means that the statements within the loop will be executed once, before the condition is tested. If the condition is false, the statements will then be repeated UNTIL the condition becomes true.

The format of the REPEAT..UNTIL structure is

```
REPEAT
   statement,
   statement
   :
UNTIL condition is true
```

As can be seen, REPEAT..UNTIL is a trailing decision loop; the statements are executed once, before the condition is tested.

There are two other considerations about which a programmer needs to be aware, before using REPEAT..UNTIL:

1 REPEAT..UNTIL loops are executed when the condition is *false*. It is only when the condition becomes *true*, that repetition ceases. Thus, the logic of the condition clause of the REPEAT..UNTIL structure is the opposite of DOWHILE:

   For instance:

   DOWHILE more records is equivalent to
   REPEAT..UNTIL no more records; and

   DOWHILE number not = 99 is equivalent to
   REPEAT.. UNTIL number = 99.

2 The statements within a REPEAT..UNTIL structure will always be executed at least once. As a result, there is no need for a *priming read* when using REPEAT..UNTIL. One read statement at the beginning of the loop is sufficient.

Let us now compare an algorithm, which uses a DOWHILE structure, with the same problem using a REPEAT..UNTIL structure.

Consider the following DOWHILE loop:

```
Process-Student-Records
   Set student-count to zero
   Read student record
   DOWHILE student number not = 999
      Write student record
      Increment student-count
      Read student record
   ENDDO
   Print student-count
END
```

This can be rewritten (incorrectly) as a trailing decision loop, using the REPEAT..UNTIL structure as follows:

```
Process-Student-Records
   Set student-count to zero
   REPEAT
      Read student record                    INCORRECT
      Write student record                   REPEAT..UNTIL logic
      Increment student-count
   UNTIL student number = 999
   Print student-count
END
```

This algorithm is incorrect, because the statements within the loop will be repeated just one time too many! Instead of immediately terminating the repetition once the trailer record has been read (Read student record), there are two more statements in the loop which will be executed, before the condition is tested. To avoid this, logic must be included which will prevent the processing of data, once the trailer record has been read. This logic takes the form of an IF statement, immediately after the Read, as follows:

```
Process-Student-Records
   Set student-count to zero
   REPEAT
      Read student record
      IF student number not = 999 THEN
         Write student record                CORRECT
         Increment student-count             REPEAT..UNTIL logic
      ENDIF
   UNTIL student number = 999
   Print student-count
END
```

REPEAT..UNTIL loops are used less frequently in pseudocode than DOWHILE loops for sequential file processing because of this extra IF statement required within the loop.

The majority of examples given in this book will use the DOWHILE construct in preference to REPEAT..UNTIL, because of its simplicity of structure. However, the following programming example does use REPEAT..UNTIL.

Example 5.4 Process inventory records

A program is required to read a series of inventory records which contain item number, item description and stock figure. The last record in the file has an item number of zero. The program is to produce a 'Low Stock Items' Report, by printing only those records which have a stock figure of less than 20 items. A heading is to print at the top of the report and a total low stock item count to print at the end.

a Defining diagram

INPUT	*PROCESSING*	*OUTPUT*
Inventory record containing:	Print Heading for each inventory record	Heading 'Low Stock Items' Inventory List containing
item number	read record	item number
item description	print record	item description
stock figure	increment Total-Low-Stock Items	stock figure
		Total-Low-Stock-Items
	print Total-Low-Stock-Items	

The programmer will need to consider the following requirements when establishing a solution algorithm:

- a REPEAT..UNTIL to perform the repetition (a DOWHILE could also have been used),
- an IF statement to select stock figures of less than 20,
- an accumulator for Total-Low-Stock-Items, and
- an extra IF, within the REPEAT loop, to ensure the trailer record is not processed.

b Solution algorithm, using REPEAT..UNTIL

```
Process-inventory-records
   Set Total-Low-Stock-Items to zero
   Print 'Low-Stock Items' Heading
   REPEAT
      Read inventory record
      IF item number > zero THEN
         IF stock figure < 20 THEN
            print item number, item description, stock figure
            increment Total-Low-Stock-Items
         ENDIF
      ENDIF
   UNTIL item number = zero
   Print Total-Low-Stock-Items
END
```

The solution algorithm has a simple structure, with a single read statement at the beginning of the REPEAT..UNTIL loop and an extra IF statement within the loop to ensure the trailer record is not incorrectly incremented into the Total-Low-Stock-Items accumulator.

The solution algorithm will now be represented by a DOWHILE structure:

b Solution algorithm, using DOWHILE

```
Process-inventory-records
   Set Total-Low-Stock-Items to zero
   Print 'Low Stock Items' Heading
   Read inventory record
   DOWHILE item number > zero
      IF stock figure < 20 THEN
         print item number, item description, stock figure
         increment Total-Low-Stock-Items
      ENDIF
      Read inventory record
   ENDDO
   Print Total-Low-Stock-Items
END
```

This solution, using DOWHILE, also has simple structure, with a priming read, and a read at the end of the loop, just before ENDDO. When a record containing an item number of zero is read, the DOWHILE condition will become false and the looping will cease.

c Desk checking

The first solution algorithm which uses REPEAT..UNTIL will be the algorithm which is desk checked. Two valid records, plus a trailer record (item number equal to zero) will be used to test the algorithm:

(i) Input Data:

	First Record	Second Record	Trailer Record
item number	123	124	0
stock figure	8	25	

(ii) Expected Result:

Heading 'Low Stock Items'
123 8 (first record)
Total Low Stock Items = 1

(iii) Desk Check Table:

	item No.	stock figure	Total-Low-Stock-Items	REPEAT Condition?	Record Printed	Heading Printed
Init Total			0			
Print Heading						Yes
REPEAT						
Read inv. record	123	8				
IF item number > 0						
IF stock figure < 20			1		Yes	
UNTIL condition				false		
Read inv. record	124	25				
IF item number > 0						
If stock figure < 20					No	
UNTIL condition				false		
Read inv. record	0					
IF item number > 0						
UNTIL condition				true		
Print-Total-Low-Stock-Items			Print			

5.3 Counted repetition constructs

Counted repetition occurs when the exact number of loop iterations is known in advance. The execution of the loop is controlled by a loop index, and instead of using DOWHILE, or REPEAT..UNTIL, the simple keyword DO is used.

```
DO loop-index = initial-value to final-value
   statement block
ENDDO
```

The DO loop does more than just repeat the statement block. It will

1 initialize the loop-index to the required initial-value;
2 increment the loop-index by 1, for each pass through the loop;
3 test the value of loop-index at the beginning of each loop to ensure that it is within the stated range of values; and
4 terminate the loop when the loop-index has exceeded the specified final-value.

In other words, a counted repetition construct will perform the initializing, incrementing and testing of the loop counter automatically. It will also terminate the loop once the required number of repetitions have been executed. In view of these properties, a counted repetition construct should be used wherever appropriate.

Example 5.5 Print student list

A program is required to read a file of 350 student records containing name, address, sex and age and to produce a STUDENT LIST. If a student is over 40 years of age, then an asterisk '*' is to be printed beside that student's details. A total of the number of students over 40 years of age is also to be printed at the end of the report.

a Defining diagram

INPUT	*PROCESSING*	*OUTPUT*
350 student records: name address sex age	Print Heading For each student: read record print details print '*' increment Total-Students-Over-40 Print Total-Students-Over-40	Heading 'STUDENT LIST' Student Details containing: name address sex age Total-Students-Over-40

b Solution algorithm

This is an example of a counted repetition loop. The problem statement indicates that the file contains exactly 350 records. So, the algorithm should contain a DO loop to control the repetition.

```
Print-student-list
   Print 'STUDENT LIST' Heading
   Set Total-Students-Over-40 to zero
   DO loop-index = 1 to 350
      read student record
      print student details
      IF age > 40 THEN
         print '*'
         increment Total-Students-Over-40
      ENDIF
   ENDDO
   Print Total-Students-Over-40
END
```

Note that the DO loop controls all the repetition:

- it initializes the loop-index to 1;
- it increments the loop-index by 1 for each pass through the loop;
- it tests the loop-index at the beginning of each pass to ensure it is within the range 1–350; and
- it automatically terminates the loop once the loop-index has exceeded 350.

c Desk checking

Two valid records should be sufficient to test the algorithm for correctness. It is not necessary to check the DO loop construct for all 350 records.

(i) **Input Data:**

	First Record	Second Record
name	J Smith	P Smith
age	30	45

(ii) **Expected Result:**

'Student List'
J Smith 30
P Smith 45 *
Total Students Over 40 1

(iii) **Desk Check Table:**

Statement	Total-Students-over-40	Loop Index	Name	Age	Print Student	Print *
Print Heading						
Initialize	0					
DO Loop Index		1				
Read student			J Smith	30		
Print student					Yes	
If age > 40						No
DO Loop Index		2				
Read student			P Smith	45		
Print student					Yes	
If age > 40	1					Yes
DO Loop Index		End				
Print Total	Print					

Desk checking the algorithm with the two input test cases has indicated that the expected results have been achieved.

5.4 Chapter summary

This chapter covered the repetition control structure in detail. Descriptions and pseudocode examples were given for DOWHILE, REPEAT..UNTIL, and counted repetition loops. Several solution algorithms which used each of the three control structures were defined, developed and desk checked.

It was noticed that all the solution algorithms which were developed to process sequential files had the same general pattern. This pattern consisted of:

1 some initial processing before the loop;
2 some processing for each record within the loop; and
3 some final processing once the loop has been exited.

Expressed as a solution algorithm using the DOWHILE construct this basic pattern was developed as a general solution:

```
Process-Sequential-File
    Do Initial Processing
    Read first record
    DOWHILE more records exist
        Process this record
        Read next record
    ENDDO
    Do Final Processing
END
```

5.5 Programming problems

Construct a solution algorithm for the following programming problems. Your solution should contain:

- a defining diagram
- a pseudocode algorithm or N–S diagram, and
- a desk check of the algorithm.

1 Design a program which will read a file of product records, each containing the item number, item name, the quantity sold this year and the quantity sold last year. The program is to produce a 'Product List' showing the item number, item name, and the increase or decrease in the quantity sold for each item.

2 Design a program which will read a file of 50 employee records. Each record contains the employee's number, name and weekly hours worked. If the employee has worked more than 35 hours in that week, then his number, name, and hours worked in excess of 35, are to be printed on a weekly 'Overtime Report'. At the end of the report, print the total overtime hours worked that week.

3 The first record of a set of records contains a bank account number and an opening balance. Each of the remaining records in the set contains the amount of a cheque drawn on that bank account. The trailer record contains a zero amount. Design a program which will read and print the account number and opening balance on a 'Statement of Account' report. The rest of the amounts are to be

read and printed on the report, each with a new running balance. A closing balance is to print at the end of the report.

4 Design a program which will read a file of employee records containing employee number, employee name, hourly pay rate, regular hours worked and overtime hours worked. The company pays its employees weekly according to the following rules:

1 Regular pay = regular hours worked × hourly rate of pay
2 Overtime pay = overtime hours worked × hourly rate of pay × 1.5
3 Total pay = regular pay + overtime pay

Your program is to read the input data on each employee's record and compute and print the employee's total pay, on the 'Weekly Payroll Report'. All input data and calculated amounts are to appear on the report. A total payroll amount is to appear at the end of the report.

CHAPTER 6

PSEUDOCODE ALGORITHMS USING SEQUENCE, SELECTION AND REPETITION

Objective

- To develop solution algorithms to eight typical programming problems using sequence, selection and repetition constructs

Outline

6.1 Eight solution algorithms

6.2 Chapter summary

6.3 Programming problems

6.1 Eight solution algorithms

The purpose of this chapter is to develop solution algorithms to eight programming problems of increasing complexity. All the algorithms will use a combination of sequence, selection and repetition constructs. Reading these algorithms should consolidate the groundwork which has been developed in the previous five chapters.

Each programming problem will be defined, the control structures required will be determined and a solution algorithm will be devised.

a Defining the problem

It is extremely important that the problem is divided into its three components: input, output and processing. The processing component should list the tasks to be performed, ie *what* needs to be done, not *how*. The verbs in each problem have been italicised, to help identify the actions to be performed.

b The control structures required

Once the problem has been defined the programmer should write down the control structures (sequence, selection and repetition) which may be needed as well as any extra variables which the solution may require.

c The solution algorithm

Having defined the problem and determined the required control structures, the programmer can devise a solution algorithm, and represent it using pseudocode. It should be understood that the solution algorithm presented in this chapter for each problem is only *one* solution to the problem. Many different and varied solutions could be equally as correct. N–S diagram solutions have not been provided.

d Desk checking

It will be the task of the reader of this book to desk check each of the algorithms with two or more test cases.

Example 6.1 Print student records

A file of student records consists of 'S' records and 'U' records. An 'S' record contains the student's number, name, age, address and attendance pattern (F/T or P/T). A 'U' record contains the number and name of the unit or units in which the student has enrolled. There may be more than one 'U' record for each 'S' record. Design a solution algorithm which will *read* the file of student records and *print* only the student's number, name and address on a 'STUDENT LIST'.

a Defining diagram

INPUT	*PROCESSING*	*OUTPUT*
Student records	Print heading	Heading 'STUDENT LIST'
'S' records	For each record	Selected student records
'U' records	read record	containing:
	print selected record	student number
		name
		address

b Control structures required

1 A DOWHILE loop to control the repetition, and
2 An IF statement to select 'S' records.

c Solution algorithm

```
Print-Student-Records
    Print 'STUDENT LIST' heading
    Read student record
    DOWHILE more records exist
        IF student record = 'S' record THEN
            print student number, name, address
        ENDIF
        Read student record
    ENDDO
END
```

Example 6.2 Print selected students

Design a solution algorithm which will *read* the same student file as in Example 6.1, and *produce* a report of all female students who are enrolled part time. The report is to be headed 'PART TIME FEMALE

STUDENTS' and is to show the student's number, name, address and age.

a Defining diagram

INPUT	*PROCESSING*	*OUTPUT*
Student records	Print heading	Heading
'S' records	For each record	Selected student records
'U' records	read record	containing:
	print selected record	student number
		name
		address
		age

b Control structures required

1 A DOWHILE loop to control the repetition, and
2 An IF statement or statements to select 'S', Female and P/T students.

c Solution algorithm

Several algorithms for this problem will be presented and all are equally correct. The only place the algorithms differ is in the expression of the IF statement. It is interesting to compare the three different solutions.

Solution a uses a non-linear nested IF:

```
Produce-Part-Time-Female-List
   Print 'PART TIME FEMALE STUDENTS'
   Read student record
   DOWHILE more records
      IF student record = 'S' record THEN
         IF attendance-pattern = P/T THEN
            IF sex = female THEN
               Write student number, name, address, age
            ENDIF
         ENDIF
      ENDIF
      Read student record
   ENDDO
END
```

Solution b uses a nested and compound IF statement:

```
Produce-Part-Time-Female-List
   Print 'PART TIME FEMALE STUDENTS'
   Read student record
   DOWHILE more records
      IF student record = 'S' record THEN
         IF (attendance-pattern = P/T
         AND sex = female) THEN
            Write student number, name, address, age
         ENDIF
      ENDIF
      Read student record
   ENDDO
END
```

Solution c also uses a compound IF statement:

```
Produce-Part-Time-Female-List
   Print 'PART TIME FEMALE STUDENTS'
   Read student record
   DOWHILE more records
      IF student record = 'S' record
      AND attendance-pattern = P/T
      AND sex = female THEN
         Write student number, name, address, age
      ENDIF
      Read student record
   ENDDO
END
```

Example 6.3 Print and total selected students

Design a solution algorithm which will *read* the same student file as in Example 6.2 and *produce* the same 'PART TIME FEMALE STUDENTS' report. In addition, you are to *print* at the end of the report the number of students who have been selected and listed, and the total number of students on the file.

a Defining diagram

INPUT	*PROCESSING*	*OUTPUT*
Student records	Print heading	Heading
'S' records	For each record	Selected student records
'U' records	read record	containing:
	print selected record	student number
	increment Total-Selected-Students	name
		address
	increment Total-Students	age
	Print Totals	Total-Selected-Students
		Total-Students

b Control structures required

1 A DOWHILE loop to control the repetition,
2 IF statements to select 'S', Female and P/T students, and
3 Accumulators for Total-Selected-Students, Total-Students.

c Solution algorithm

```
Produce-Part-Time-Female-List
    Print 'PART TIME FEMALE STUDENTS'
    Set Total-Students to zero
    Set Total-Selected-Students to zero
    Read student record
    DOWHILE records exist
        IF student record = 'S' record THEN
            increment Total-Students
            IF (attendance-pattern = P/T
            AND sex = female) THEN
                increment Total-Selected-Students
                Print student number, name, address, age
            ENDIF
        ENDIF
        Read student record
    ENDDO
    Print Total-Students
    Print Total-Selected-Students
END
```

Note the positions where the Total accumulators are incremented. If these statements are not placed accurately within their respective IF statements, then the algorithm could produce erroneous results.

Example 6.4 Produce Sales Report

Design a program which will *read* a file of sales records and *produce* a sales report. The first record in the file contains the number of records in the file (N). Every other record in the file contains a customer's number, name, a sales amount and a discount code.

The discount code is to be *applied* to the sales amount to *determine* the discount due on that sale, as follows:

Discount Code	*Discount*
0	nil discount
1	3% discount
2	5% discount

This report is to *print* a heading 'SALES REPORT' and detail lines *listing* the customer number, name, sales amount, discount and total amount due for the customer.

a Defining diagram

INPUT	*PROCESSING*	*OUTPUT*
First record (N)	Read N	Heading
Sales records	For each record	Detail Lines
cust-number	read record	cust-number
name	calculate discount	name
sales-amt	calculate Total-amt	sales-amt
disc-code	print details	discount
		Total-amt

b Control structures required

1 A DO loop, to control the repetition N times.
2 A *case* statement to calculate the discount.
3 It is assumed in this problem that the disc-code field has been validated, and will only contain a value of 0, 1 or 2.

c Solution algorithm

```
Produce-Sales-Report
   Print 'SALES REPORT' Heading
   Read first record (N)
   DO loop-index = 1 to N
      read sales record
      CASE OF disc-code
         0 : discount = 0
         1 : discount = sales-amt * 0.03
         2 : discount = sales-amt * 0.05
      ENDCASE
      Total-amt = sales-amt - discount
      Print customer number, name, sales-amt, discount,
      Total-amt
   ENDDO
END
```

A linear nested IF statement could have been used in place of the *case* statement in this example. The *case* statement, however, expresses the logic so simply, that it should be used wherever appropriate.

Example 6.5 Student test results

Design a solution algorithm which will *read* a file of student test results and produce a Student Test Grades report. Each test record contains the student number, name and test score (out of 50). The program is to *calculate* for each student the percentage of correct test answers and to *print* the student's number, name, test score and letter grade on the report. The letter grade is *determined* as follows:

A	=	90%	—	100%
B	=	80%	—	89%
C	=	70%	—	79%
D	=	60%	—	69%
F	=	0%	—	59%

a Defining diagram

INPUT	PROCESSING	OUTPUT
Student Test Results	Print Heading	Heading
student-number	For each student:	Student details
name	read record	containing:
test-score	calculate percentage	student-number
	calculate grade	name
	print details	test-score
		grade

b Control structures required

1 A DOWHILE loop to control the repetition.
2 A linear nested IF statement to calculate the grade. (Note: the *case* construct cannot be used here, as it is not designed to cater for a range of values — eg 0%–59%).
3 A formula to calculate the percentage.

c Solution algorithm

```
Print-student-results
    Print 'STUDENT TEST GRADES' Heading
    Read student record
    DOWHILE not EOF
        percentage = test-score * 2
        IF percentage > 89% THEN
            grade = A
        ELSE
            IF percentage > 79% THEN
                grade = B
            ELSE
                IF percentage > 69% THEN
                    grade = C
                ELSE
                    IF percentage > 59% THEN
                        grade = D
                    ELSE
                        grade = F
                    ENDIF
                ENDIF
            ENDIF
        ENDIF
        Print student-number, name, test-score, grade
        Read student record
    ENDDO
END
```

Note that the linear nested IF has been worded so that all alternatives have been considered.

Example 6.6 Gas supply billing

The Domestic Gas Supply Company records its customers' gas usage figures on a Customer Usage File. Each record on the file contains the customer number, customer name, customer address and gas usage expressed in cubic metres.

The company bills its customers according to the following rate: If the customer's usage is 60 cubic metres or less, a rate of £2.00 per cubic metre is applied. If the customer's usage is more than 60 cubic metres, then a rate of £1.75 per cubic metre is applied for the first 60 cubic metres, and a rate of £1.50 is applied for the remaining usage.

Design a solution algorithm which will *read* the Customer Usage File and *produce* a report listing each customer's number, name, address, gas usage and the amount owing.

At the end of the report, *print* the total number of customers and the total amount owing to the company.

a Defining diagram

INPUT	*PROCESSING*	*OUTPUT*
Customer usage:	Print Report Heading	Print Report Heading
customer-number	For each customer:	Customer details:
name	Read record	customer-number
address	Calculate amount-owing	name
gas-usage	Print customer details	address
	Increment Total-Customers	gas-usage
	Increment Total-Amount-Owing	amount-owing
	Print Total-Customers	Total-Customers
	Print Total-Amount-Owing	Total-Amount-Owing

b Control structures required

1 A DOWHILE loop to control the repetition.
2 IF statements to calculate amount-owing.
3 Accumulators for Total-Customers, Total-Amount-Owing.

c Solution algorithm

```
Bill-gas-customers
    Print 'CUSTOMER USAGE FIGURES' Heading
    Set Total-Customers to zero
    Set Total-Amount-Owing to zero
    Read customer record
    DOWHILE more records
        IF usage < = 60 metres THEN
            amount-owing = usage * £2.00
        ELSE
            amount-owing = (60 * £1.75) + ((usage - 60) * £1.50)
        ENDIF
        Print customer-number, name, address, gas-usage,
                amount-owing
        Add amount-owing to Total-Amount-Owing
        Add 1 to Total-Customers
        Read customer record
    ENDDO
    Print Total-Customers
    Print Total-Amount-Owing
END
```

Example 6.7 Electricity usage report

An Electricity Supply Authority records its customers' Usage Figures on an Electricity Usage File. This file consists of:

1 A header record (first record) which provides the total kilowatt hours used during the month, by all customers.
2 A number of detail records, each containing the customer number, customer name and electricity usage in kilowatt hours for the month.

Design a solution algorithm which will *read* the Electricity Usage File and *produce* an 'ELECTRICITY USAGE' report showing the customer's number, name, customer usage figure and amount owing. The amount owing is *calculated* at 11 pence for each kilowatt hour used up to 200 hours and 8 pence for each kilowatt hour over 200 hours. The total customer usage in kilowatt hours is also to be *accumulated*.

At the end of the program *compare* the total customer usage which was accumulated in the program with the value provided in the header record, and *print* an appropriate message if the totals are not equal.

a Defining diagram

INPUT	*PROCESSING*	*OUTPUT*
Header record	Print Heading	Heading
Header-usage	Read Header Record	Customer Details
Customer records:	For each customer:	containing:
customer-number	read record	customer-number
name	calculate amount-owing	name
customer-usage	increment Total-usage	customer-usage
	print customer details	amount-owing
	Compare Total-usage to Header-usage	Error message
	Print message	

b Control structures required

1. A DOWHILE loop to control the repetition.
2. An IF statement to calculate amount-owing.
3. An accumulator for Total-usage.
4. An IF statement to compare Header-usage with Total-usage.

c Solution algorithm

```
Print-Electricity-Usage-report
    Print 'ELECTRICITY USAGE' Heading
    Set Total-usage to zero
    Read header record for Header-usage
    Read customer record
    DOWHILE more records
        IF customer-usage <= 200 THEN
            amount-owing = customer-usage * 11
        ELSE
            amount-owing = (200 * 11) + ((customer-usage – 200) * 8)
        ENDIF
        Divide amount-owing by 100 (convert to £)
        Print customer-number, name, customer-usage, amount-owing
        Add customer-usage to Total-usage
        Read customer record
    ENDDO
    IF Total-usage NOT = Header-usage THEN
        Print appropriate message
    ENDIF
END
```

Note that, in this example, there is:

- initial processing before the loop;
- processing of the current record within the loop; and
- final processing after exiting the loop.

Example 6.8 Process payroll earnings

Design a solution algorithm which will *read* a file of payroll earning records and *produce* a summary report of those records. Each record contains a record code, employee number, employee name, and earnings in pounds and pence. The record code indicates the type of payment which has been made to the employee, as follows:

Record code	*Payment*
1	Regular pay
2	Overtime pay
3	Extra shift
4	Bonus

Your program is to *count* the number of each type of record and *accumulate* the total earnings for each type. A two-line 'PAYMENT SUMMARY' report is to be *produced* showing the count and total earnings for each record type.

Records with invalid record codes are to be *counted* but the earnings for these codes are not to be accumulated.

a Defining diagram

INPUT	*PROCESSING*	*OUTPUT*
Payroll record:	Print Heading	Heading
record-code	For each record:	record type counts
emp-no	read record	Tot-Earnings
emp-name	Accumulate record type counts	
earnings	Accumulate Tot-Earnings	
	Print record type counts	
	Print Tot-Earnings	

b Control structures required

1 A DOWHILE structure to control the repetition.
2 A *case* statement to accumulate record type counts and earnings.
3 Accumulators for record type counts and record type earnings.

c Solution algorithm

```
Process-Payroll-Earnings
   Print 'PAYMENT SUMMARY' Heading
   Print record type column headings (1,2,3,4,Invalid)
   Set Count1, Count2, Count3, Count4, Count-Invalid to zero
   Set Tot-Earnings1, Tot-Earnings2, Tot-Earnings3, Tot-Earnings4
      to zero
   Read Payroll Record
   DOWHILE not EOF
      CASE OF record-code
         1      : increment Count1
                  add earnings to Tot-Earnings1
         2      : increment Count2
                  add earnings to Tot-Earnings2
         3      : increment Count3
                  add earnings to Tot-Earnings3
         4      : increment Count4
                  add earnings to Tot-Earnings4
         other  : increment Count-Invalid
      ENDCASE
      Read Payroll Record
   ENDDO
   Print Count1, Count2, Count3, Count4, Count-Invalid
   Print Tot-Earnings1, Tot-Earnings2, Tot-Earnings3, Tot-Earnings4
END
```

6.2 Chapter summary

This chapter developed solution algorithms to eight typical programming problems. The approach to all eight problems followed the same path:

- The problem was defined, using a defining diagram.
- The control structures required were written down, along with any extra variables required.
- The solution algorithm was produced, using pseudocode and the three basic control structures: sequence, selection and repetition.

It was noted that all the solution algorithms followed the same basic pattern, although the statements within that pattern were quite different. This pattern was first introduced in Chapter 5, as follows:

```
Process-Sequential-File
   DO Initial Processing
   Read first record
   DOWHILE more records exist
      Process this record
      Read next record
   ENDDO
   DO Final Processing
END
```

6.3 Programming problems

Construct a solution algorithm for the following programming problems. Your solution should contain:

- a defining diagram,
- a list of control structures required,
- a pseudocode algorithm, and
- a desk check of the algorithm.

1 A parts inventory record contains the following fields:
   - record code, (only code 11 is valid)
   - part number (6 characters; 2 alpha and 4 numeric, eg. AA1234)
   - part description, and
   - inventory balance.

   Design a program which will read a file of parts inventory records and print the contents of all the valid inventory records with a zero inventory balance.

2 Design a program which will read the same parts inventory file described in problem 1 and print the details of all valid records whose part numbers fall within the values AA3000 and AA3999 inclusive. Your program is also required to print a count of these selected records at the end of the parts listing.

3 Design a program which will produce the same report as in problem 2, but in addition, print at the end of the parts listing, a count of all the records whose part number begins with the value 'AA'.

4 Design a program which will read a file of customer credit account balances and produce a report showing the customer's minimum amount due. Each customer record contains the customer number, name, address, postcode and total amount owing.

The minimum amount due is calculated to be one-quarter of the total amount owing, provided this calculated amount is not less than £5.00. At least £5.00 must be paid when the total amount owing is greater than £5.00. If the total amount owing is less than £5.00 then the total amount is payable.

5 A file of student records contains name, sex (M or F), age (in years) and marital status (single or married). Design a program to read through the file and compute the numbers of married men, single men, married women and single women. Print these numbers on a 'STUDENT SUMMARY' report. If any single men are over 30 years of age, print their names on a separate 'SINGLE MEN' report.

CHAPTER 7

MODULARIZATION

Objectives

- To introduce modularization as a means of dividing a problem into subtasks
- To present hierarchy charts as a pictorial representation of modular program structure
- To develop programming examples which use a modularized structure

Outline

7.1 Modularization

Throughout the previous six chapters, it has been emphasized that to design a solution algorithm, a programmer must:

- define the problem;
- write down the control structures required to reach a solution; and
- devise a solution algorithm, which uses a combination of sequence, selection and repetition control structures.

Many solution algorithms have been presented, and all have been relatively simple; the finished algorithm has been less than one page in length. As programming problems increase in complexity, however, it becomes more and more difficult to consider the solution as a whole. Given a complex problem, a programmer cannot often see, initially, what the solution might be. So he or she must first identify the major tasks to be performed in the problem, and then divide the problem into sections which represent those tasks. These sections can be considered subtasks or functions. Once the major tasks in the problem have been identified the programmer may then need to look at each of the subtasks and identify within them further subtasks, and so on. This process of identifying first the major tasks and then further subtasks within them is known as top-down design.

By using this top-down design methodology the programmer is adopting a modular approach to program design. That is, each of the subtasks or functions will eventually become a module within a solution algorithm or program. A *module,* then, can be defined as a section of an algorithm which is dedicated to a single function. The use of modules makes the algorithm simpler, more systematic, and more likely to be free of errors. Since each module represents a single task, the programmer can develop the solution algorithm task by task, or module by module, until the complete solution has been devised.

The division of a problem into smaller subtasks, or modules is a simple process. The programmer, when defining the problem, writes down the activities or processing steps to be performed. These activities are grouped together to form more manageable tasks or functions, and these functions will eventually form modules. The emphasis when defining the problem will still concentrate on *what* tasks or functions need to be performed. Each function will be made up of a number of activities, all of which contribute to the performance of a single task.

A module must be large enough to perform its task, and must include only the operations which contribute to the performance of that task. It should have a single entry, and a single exit with a top-to-bottom sequence of instructions. The name of the module should describe the work to be done as a single specific function. The convention of naming a module by using a verb, followed by a two-word object is particularly important here, as it helps to identify the separate task or function which it has been designed to perform. For example, typical module names might be:

```
Print-Page-Headings
Calculate-Sales-Tax
Validate-Input-Date
```

By using meaningful module names such as these, a programmer can automatically describe the task that the module has been designed to perform.

The mainline

Since each module performs a single specific task, a *mainline* routine must provide the master control which ties all the modules together and co-ordinates their activity. This program mainline should show the main processing functions, and the order in which they are to be performed. It should also show the flow of data and the major control structures. The mainline should be easy to read, be of manageable length and show sound logic structure. Generally, a programmer should be able to read a pseudocode mainline, and see exactly what is being done in the program. Let us look at a pseudocode mainline for a program which produces bills for patients upon their discharge from hospital. The program is named Create-Patient-Bill and the processing steps which are underlined, represent the modules which are called from the mainline.

```
Create-Patient-Bill
    Initialize charges fields
    Read patient charges record
    DOWHILE patient records exist
        Compute-Accommodation-Charges
        Compute-Theatre-Charges
        Compute-Pathology-Charges
        Compute-Sundries-Charges
        Write-Patient-Bill
        Read patient charges record
    ENDDO
    Print total patients, total charges
END
```

This mainline has exactly the same basic pattern as all our other solution algorithms. The first patient record is read before the loop; that record is processed within the loop; and the next record is read at the end of the loop. When there are no more records in the file, the repetition will stop, and control will pass to the statement after ENDDO. (Print total patients, total charges.)

However, instead of performing all the activities itself, this mainline calls on a series of modules to perform the tasks. The mainline will pass control to a module which will *perform* a task. When the module has reached its end it will pass control back to the mainline, which will then pass control to the next module and so on.

Note that the name of each module describes the specific function for which it is intended. Without knowing the contents of any of the modules, a programmer can read this mainline and obtain a good idea of what is happening in the program.

7.2 Hierarchy charts or structure charts

After all the tasks have been grouped into modules, the programmer should present these modules graphically in a diagram. This diagram is known as a hierarchy chart as it shows not only the names of all the modules, but also their hierarchical relationship to each other.

In other texts a hierarchy chart may be referred to as a structure chart or a visual Table of Contents. The hierarchy chart uses a tree like diagram of boxes; each box represents a module in the program and, the lines connecting the boxes represent the relationship of the modules to others in the program hierarchy. The chart shows no particular sequence of processing of the modules; only the modules themselves in the order in which they first appear in the algorithm.

At the top of the hierarchy chart is the controlling module, or mainline. On the next level are all the modules which are called directly from the mainline; that is the modules immediately *subordinate* to the mainline. On the next level are the modules which are subordinate to the modules on the first level, and so on. This chart form of hierarchical relationship appears similar to an organizational chart of personnel within a large company.

Let us now look at the hierarchy chart for the program Create–Patient–Bill as developed so far.

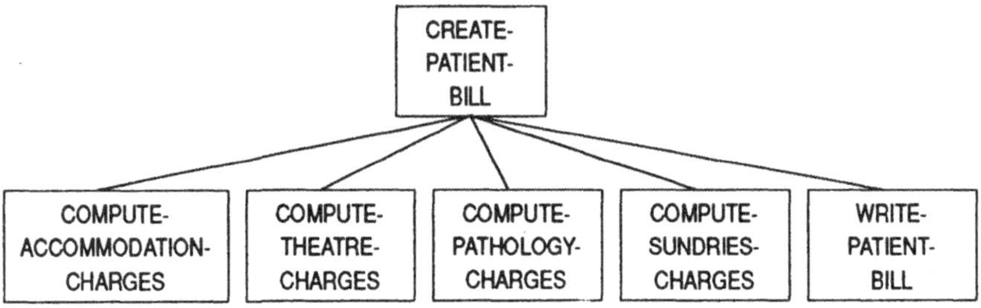

The mainline will pass control to each module when it is ready for that module to perform its task. The controlling module is said to *invoke* or *call* the subordinate module. The controlling module is, therefore, referred to as the *calling* module, and the subordinate module the *called* module. On completion of its task, the called module returns control to the calling module.

One of the called modules may itself call other subordinate modules. The 'Compute-Theatre-Charges' module may need to call other modules to help it complete its task. It may call, for example, three modules, named:

Calculate-Doctors-Charges;
Calculate-Anaesthetists-Charges; and
Calculate-Facilities-Charges.

Similarly, 'Compute-Sundries-Charges' may need to call two other modules named:

Calculate-TV-Charges; and
Calculate-Telephone-Charges.

When we add these new modules to the next level of the hierarchy chart it could look like this:

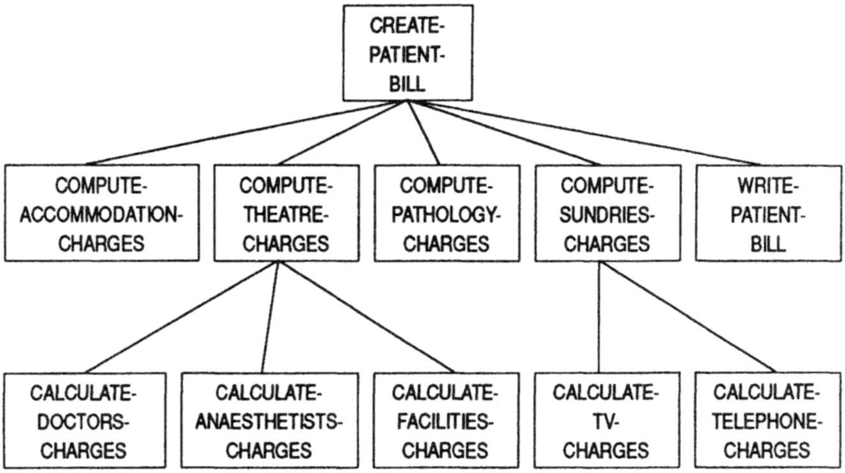

As a general rule, no module should have more than seven modules subordinate to it. Using more than seven modules is an indication that the programmer may be considering too many subtasks at once.

7.3 Steps in modularization

Top-down modular design is really quite simple if the following steps are performed every time a programmer is presented with a programming problem:

1 *Define* the problem by dividing it into its three components: input, output and processing. The processing component should consist of a list of activities to be performed.

2 *Group* the activities into subtasks or functions to determine the modules which will make up the program. Remember that a module is one section of a program dedicated to the performance of a single function. Note that not all the activities may be identified at this stage. Only the modules of the first level of the hierarchy chart may be identified, with other more subordinate modules developed later.

3 *Construct* a hierarchy chart to illustrate the modules, and their relationship to each other. Once the structure (or organization) of the program has been developed, the order of processing of the modules can be considered.

4 *Establish* the logic of the mainline of the algorithm in pseudocode. This mainline should contain some initial processing before the loop; some processing of the record within the loop; and some final processing after exiting the loop. It should contain calls to the major processing modules of the program, and should be easy to read and understand.

5 *Develop* the pseudocode for each successive module in the hierarchy chart. The modularization process is complete when the pseudocode for each module on the lowest level of the hierarchy chart has been developed.

6 *Desk check* the solution algorithm. This is achieved by first desk checking the mainline, and then each subordinate module in turn.

7.4 Programming examples using modules

The solution algorithms to the following programming examples will be developed using the six steps in modularization, introduced in section 7.3.

Example 7.1 Produce orders report

The Acme Spare Parts Company wants to produce an 'Orders Report' from its Product Orders File. Each record on the file contains the product number of the product ordered; the product description; the number of units ordered; the retail price per unit; the freight charges per unit; and the packaging costs per unit.

The output report is to contain headings and column headings as specified in the chart below. Each detail line is to contain the product number, description, number of units ordered and the Total Amount Due for the order. There is to be an allowance of 45 detail lines per page.

The amount due for each product is the number of units ordered times the retail price of the unit. A discount of 10% is allowed on the amount due for all orders over £100.00. The freight charges and packaging costs per unit must be added to this resulting value to determine the Total Amount Due.

```
                        ACME SPARE PARTS           PAGE xx
                         ORDERS REPORT

  PRODUCT        PRODUCT         UNITS    TOTAL AMOUNT
    NO         DESCRIPTION      ORDERED        DUE

   xxxxx       xxxxxxxxxxx        xxx         xxxxx
   xxxxx       xxxxxxxxxxx        xxx         xxxxx
```

a Define the problem

INPUT	*PROCESSING*	*OUTPUT*
Order Record	Print Headings as required	Headings
prod-number	For each product:	main headings
prod-description	read order record	column headings
no-of-units	calculate amount-due	page number
retail-price	calculate discount	Detail Line
freight-charge	calculate freight-charge	prod-number
packaging-charge	calculate packaging	product-description
	print detail line	no-of-units
		Total-amount-due

b Group the activities into modules

The activities in the processing component can be grouped into two functions or modules as follows

1 'Print Headings as required' can become a module. This is an example of a module which will be created because it is re-usable. That is, the module will be called whenever the report needs to skip to a new page. A page headings module is a standard requirement of most report programs. The name of this module will be 'Print-Page-Headings'.

2 The four processing steps:

'calculate amount-due';
'calculate discount';
'calculate freight-charge'; and
'calculate packaging';

can be grouped together because they all contribute to the performance of a single task – to calculate the Total-amount-due. It is this Total-amount-due which is required on each detail line of the report. The name of this module will be 'Calculate-Total- Amount-Due' to describe its function.

c Construct a hierarchy chart

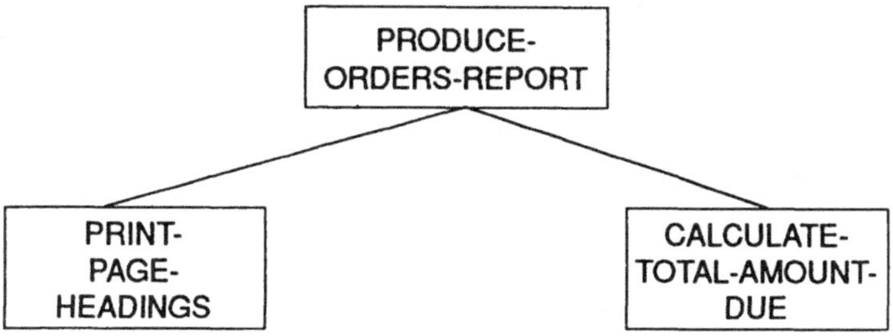

This diagram illustrates the structure of the algorithm. The main controlling module, or mainline, is called 'Produce-Orders-Report'. The mainline will call on two subordinate modules, namely 'Print-Page-Headings' and 'Calculate-Total-Amount-Due', as required. When the mainline calls on a module, it will pass control to that module. All the processing steps in the module will then be executed before control returns to the mainline.

d Establish the logic of the mainline of the algorithm. Express the solution algorithm using pseudocode

The mainline will require:

1 A DOWHILE loop to control the repetition.
2 Calls to its two subordinate modules.
3 A page accumulator for the page heading routine.

4 A line counter to record the number of detail lines printed on each page.

```
PRODUCE-ORDERS-REPORT
   Set page-counter to zero
   Print-Page-Headings
   Set line-counter to zero
   Read order record
   DOWHILE more records
      IF line-counter >= 45 THEN
         Print-Page-Headings
         Set line-counter to zero
      ENDIF
      Calculate-Total-Amount-Due
      Print prod-number, prod-description, no-of-units, and
         Total-amount-due
      Add 1 to line-counter
      Read order record
   ENDDO
END
```

Note that the calls to the modules in the mainline are highlighted by underlining the names of the modules where they appear in the mainline logic.

e Develop pseudocode for each successive module in the hierarchy chart

1 The pseudocode for 'Print-Page-Headings' is standard for a page heading routine which will increment the page counter and print a series of headings.

```
Print-Page-Headings
   Add 1 to page-counter
   Write Main Heading 'ACME SPARE PARTS'
   Write Heading 'ORDERS REPORT'
   Write Column Headings 1
   Write Column Headings 2
   Write Blank Line
END
```

2 The pseudocode for the module 'Calculate-Total-Amount-Due' will compute the total amount using a series of intermediate calculations.

```
Calculate-Total-Amount-Due
   amount-due = no-of-units * retail price
   IF amount-due > £100.00 THEN
      discount = amount-due * 0.1
   ELSE
      discount = zero
   ENDIF
   amount-due = amount-due – discount
   freight-due = freight-charge * no-of-units
   packaging-due = packaging-charge * no-of-units
   Total-amount-due = amount-due + freight-due + packaging-due
END
```

f Desk check the solution algorithm

The desk checking of an algorithm with modules is no different to the method developed for our previous examples.

1 Create some valid input test data.
2 List the output that the input data is expected to produce.
3 Use a Desk Check Table to walk the data through the *mainline* of the algorithm to ensure that the expected output is achieved.

(i) **Input Data:**
Three test cases will be used to test the algorithm. To test for correct page skipping, we could temporarily reduce the line limit from 45 to a conveniently small number, eg 2.

Record	Prod-number	Prod-description	No-of units	Retail-price	Freight-charge	Packaging-charge
1	100	Rubber Hose	10	1.00	0.20	0.50
2	200	Steel Pipe	20	2.00	0.10	0.20
3	300	Steel Bolt	100	3.00	0.10	0.20
EOF						

(ii) **Expected Output:**

ACME SPARE PARTS PAGE 1
ORDERS REPORT

PRODUCT NO	PRODUCT DESCRIPTION	UNITS ORDERED	TOTAL AMOUNT DUE
100	Rubber Hose	10	£17.00
200	Steel Pipe	20	£46.00
300	Steel Bolt	100	£300.00

(iii) Desk Check Table:

Only the processing steps of the mainline of the algorithm will be written down in the Desk Check Table. When a call is made to a module, all the processing steps in that module will be recorded on one line of the desk check table. By doing this, the internal logic of each module is checked at the same time as the mainline.

Steps	DOWHILE OK	Page count	Line count	Prod. no.	No. of units	Retail Price	Freight charge	Packing charge	Total amount	Print
Init. page-counter		0								
Print-Page-Headings		1								Headings
Init. line-counter			0							
Read order rec				100	10	1.00	0.20	0.50		
DOWHILE	Yes									
IF line-count			No							
Calc-Total-Amt-Due									17.00	
Print details										Detail line
Inc. line-counter			1							
Read order rec				200	20	2.00	0.10	0.20		
DOWHILE	Yes									
IF line-Count			No							
Calc-Total-Amt-Due									46.00	
Print details										Detail line
Inc. line-counter			2							
Read order rec				300	100	3.00	0.10	0.20		
DOWHILE	Yes									
IF line-Count			No							
Calc-Total-Amt-Due									300.00	
Print details										Detail line
Inc. line-counter			3							
Read order rec				EOF						
DOWHILE	No									
END										

Example 7.2 Calculate new vehicle cost

A program is required to calculate and print the cost of a new vehicle, after a customer has ordered the vehicle.

The program is to be interactive: that is, all the input details will be provided at a screen terminal on the salesperson's desk. The program will then calculate the related costs and return the information to the screen.

The input details required are:

Owner's Name
Vehicle Make
Vehicle Model
Body Type (Saloon, Estate, Hatchback, etc.)
Basic Price of Vehicle

Duty has to be paid on new vehicles. This is calculated at the rate of 8.33% on the basic price of the vehicle. The dealer adds an 'On-the-Road' fee to cover delivery, number plates, road tax, etc. This is calculated as 5% of the basic price of the vehicle, up to a maximum charge of £750. Once all the charges have been calculated and added to the basic price, Value Added Tax must be added at the rate of 17.5%, to give the total amount payable by the customer.

The program is to make all these calculations and then print the information on the screen as follows:

Duty
On-the-Road fee
Total Pre-VAT charges
Total Pre-VAT price
VAT
Total amount payable

The program is to process vehicle costs until an owner's name of 'XXX' is entered. None of the other entry details will be required after the value 'XXX' has been entered.

a Define the problem

INPUT	*PROCESSING*	*OUTPUT*
Owners-Name	For each record:	Duty
Vehicle-Make	get input details	On-the-Road
Vehicle-Model	calc Duty	Pre-VAT-Charges
Body-Type	calc On-the-Road	Pre-VAT-Price
Basic-Price	calc Pre-VAT-Charges	VAT
	calc Pre-VAT-Price	Total-Amount-Payable
	calc VAT	
	calc Total-Amount-Payable	
	print information to screen	

b Group the activities into modules

The activities in the processing component can be grouped into three main functions, as follows:

1 Get input details.
There are a number of input fields to read from the screen, so a module can be created to perform this function. The name of the module will be 'Get-Vehicle-Details'. Note that the read from the screen of the owner's name must be separate, as it is the entry of 'XXX' in this field which will cause the repetition to stop.

2 Print information to screen.
Similarly, there are a number of output fields to print to the screen, so a module can be created to perform this function. The name of this module will be 'Print-Cost-Details'.

3 The activities
calc Duty
calc On-the-Road
calc Pre-VAT-Charges
calc Pre-VAT-Price
calc VAT
calc Total-Amount-Payable
all contribute to the performance of a single Task: to calculate the total amount payable. The name of this module will be 'Calculate-Total-Amount-Payable'.

This module could be subdivided to include two smaller tasks, namely 'Calculate-Pre-VAT-Charges' and 'Calculate-VAT'. If this division is made then the module 'Calculate-Total-Amount-Payable' would call these two modules to perform those functions.

c Construct a hierarchy chart

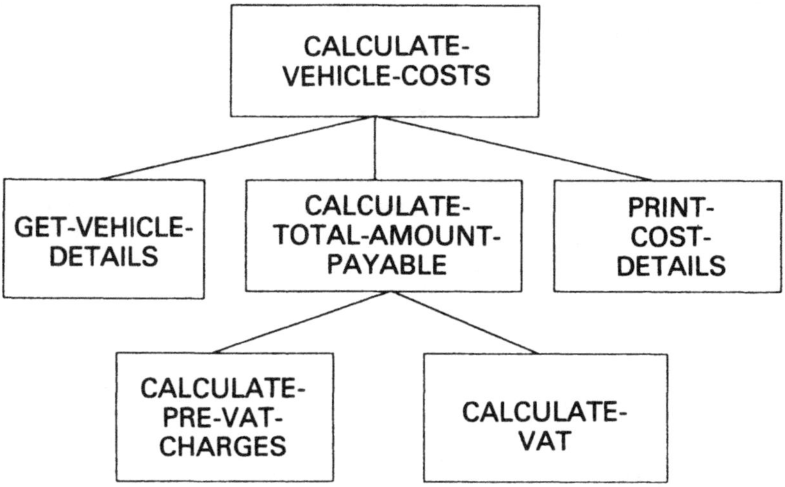

The hierarchy chart illustrates the structure that the algorithm will take. The mainline is called 'Calculate-Vehicle-Costs'. It will call three subordinate modules 'Get-Vehicle-Details', 'Calculate-Total-Amount-Payable' and 'Print-Cost-Details'. The module 'Calculate-Total-Amount-Payable' will also call two modules to help perform its task: 'Calculate-Pre-VAT-Charges' and 'Calculate-VAT'.

d Establish the logic of the mainline of the algorithm, using pseudocode

The mainline will require:

1 A DOWHILE loop to process the repetition; and
2 Calls to the modules as required.

```
CALCULATE-VEHICLE-COSTS
   Set Total-Amount-Payable to zero
   Read Owners-Name
   DOWHILE Owners-Name NOT = 'XXX'
      Get-Vehicle-Details
      Calculate-Total-Amount-Payable
      Print-Cost-Details
      Read Owners-Name
   ENDDO
END
```

Note that the mainline appears to be very simple. It consists of a read before the loop, calls to its three subordinate modules within the loop, and a read just before the end of the loop. By reading the algorithm, a programmer can easily understand the processing of the program. This is because of the modular nature of the algorithm and the careful choice of module names.

e Develop the pseudocode for each successive module in the hierarchy chart

1 'Get-Vehicle-Details' is the module which prompts for and reads the required fields. The owner's name is read separately in the mainline.

```
GET-VEHICLE-DETAILS
   Read Vehicle-Make
   Read Vehicle-Model
   Read Body-Type
   Read Basic-Price
END
```

2 'Calculate-Total-Amount-Payable' is the module which calls two other modules.

```
CALCULATE-TOTAL-AMOUNT-PAYABLE
   Calculate-Pre-VAT-Charges
   Pre-VAT-Price = Pre-VAT-Charges + Basic-Price
   Calculate-VAT
   Total-Amount-Payable = Pre-VAT-Price + VAT
END
```

3 'Calculate-Pre-VAT-Charges' contains the steps required to calculate the Duty and the On-the-Road fee. Duty is calculated at 8.33% of the Basic Price. The On-the-Road fee is calculated at 5% of the Basic Price, subject to a maximum fee of £750.

```
CALCULATE-PRE-VAT-CHARGES
   Duty = Basic-Price * 0.0833
   On-the-Road = Basic-Price * 0.05
   IF On-the-Road > 750 THEN
      On-the-Road = 750
   ENDIF
   Pre-VAT-Charges = Duty + On-the-Road
END
```

4 'Calculate-VAT' is the module which calculates the VAT payable on the vehicle. The rate of Value Added Tax is 17.5% of the basic price of the vehicle together with the other charges.

```
CALCULATE-VAT
   VAT = Pre-VAT-Price * 0.175
END
```

5 'Print-Cost-Details' is a module which prints the required output on the screen.

```
PRINT-COST-DETAILS
   Print Duty
   Print On-the-Road
   Print Total-Pre-VAT-Charges
   Print Total-Pre-VAT-Price
   Print VAT
   Print Total-Amount-Payable
END
```

When a program is modularized in this fashion, the pseudocode for each successive module becomes very simple.

f Desk check the solution algorithm

(i) Input Data:

As there are two branches in the logic of the program, two test cases should be sufficient to test the algorithm. Only the relevant input fields will be provided.

	Basic Price
Record 1	3000
Record 2	20000
'XXX'	

(ii) Expected Output

	Record 1	Record 2
Duty	250	1666
On-the-Road Fee	150	750
Total Pre-VAT-Charges	400	2416
Pre-VAT-Price	3400	22416
VAT	595	3923
Total Amount Payable	3995	26339

(iii) Desk Check Table:

The desk checking will be of the main processing steps of the mainline. When a call to a module is made, all the processing steps of the module are recorded on one line of the desk check table.

Steps	DOWHILE OK	Basic Price	Duty	On-the-Road	Pre-VAT Charges	Pre-VAT Price	VAT	Total Payable	Print Details
Read-Owners-Name	Record 1								
DOWHILE	Yes								
Get-Vehicle-Details		3000							
Calc-Total-Payable			250	150	400	3400	595	3995	
Print-Cost-Details									Yes
Read-Owners-Name	Record 2								
DOWHILE	Yes								
Get-Vehicle-Details		20 000							
Calc-Total-Payable			1666	750	2416	22 416	3923	26 339	
Print-Cost-Details									Yes
Read-Owners-Name	'XXX'								
DOWHILE	No								
END	Yes								

7.5 Chapter summary

This chapter introduced a modular approach to program design. The terms *top-down design* and *module* were defined and programming examples were provided to show the benefits of using modularization.

Hierarchy charts were introduced as a method of illustrating the structure of a program which contains modules. Hierarchy charts show the names of all the modules and their hierarchical relationship to each other.

The steps in modularization which a programmer must follow were listed. These were: define the problem; group the activities into subtasks or functions; construct a hierarchy chart; establish the logic of the mainline; develop the pseudocode for each successive module and desk check the solution algorithm.

Programming examples which used these six steps in modularization were then developed in pseudocode.

7.6 Programming problems

Construct a solution algorithm for the following programming problems. To obtain your final solution you should:

- define the problem
- group the activities into modules
- construct a hierarchy chart
- establish the logic of the mainline using pseudocode
- develop the pseudocode for each successive module in the hierarchy chart, and
- desk check the solution algorithm.

1 The Tidy Phones Telephone Company's charges file contains records for each call made by its Metroville subscribers during a month. Each record on the file contains the subscriber's name; subscriber's phone number; phone number called; distance from Metroville of the number called (in kilometres); and the duration of the call (in seconds).

Design a program which will read the Tidy Phones charges file and produce a Telephone Charges report, as follows.

```
                      TIDY PHONES
                  TELEPHONE CHARGES              PAGE XX


SUBSCRIBER   SUBSCRIBER    PHONE NUMBER    COST OF
   NAME        NUMBER         CALLED         CALL

XXXXXXXXXX   XX-XXX-XXXX   XXX-XXX-XXXX     999.99
XXXXXXXXXX   XX-XXX-XXXX   XXX-XXX-XXXX     999.99

                           TOTAL REVENUE   9999.99
```

Main headings and column headings are to appear as printed on the report with an allowance of 45 detail lines per page. The Total Revenue line is to print three lines after the last detail line.

The cost of each call is calculated as follows:

Distance from Metroville	Cost (£) /Minute
less than 25 km	0.35
25 < = km < 75	0.65
75 < = km < 300	1.00
300 < = km < = 1000	2.00
greater than 1000 km	3.00

2 The Mitre-11 hardware outlets require an inventory control program which is to accept order details for an item, and generate a Shipping List and a Back Order List.

Design an interactive program which will conduct a dialogue on the screen for the input values, and print the reports as required.

The screen dialogue is to appear as follows:

```
ENTER Item No       :  99999
   Quantity on Hand :    999
   Order quantity   :    999
   Order number     : 999999
```

If an item number does not have precisely five digits then an error message is to appear on the screen.

If the quantity on hand is sufficient to meet the order then one line is to be printed on the Shipping List.

If the quantity on hand is insufficient to meet the order, then the order is to be partially filled by whatever stock is available. For this situation one line should appear on the Shipping List with the appropriate number of units shipped and a message 'Order Partially Filled'. An entry for the balance of the order is to be printed on the Back Order List.

If the quantity on hand is zero, then the message 'OUT OF STOCK' is to appear on the Shipping List, and an entry for the full quantity ordered is to be printed on the Back Order List.

Your program is to continue to process inventory orders, until a value of zero is entered for the item number.

Report Layouts for the Shipping List and Back Order List are as follows:

MITRE-11 HARDWARE
INVENTORY CONTROL
SHIPPING LIST PAGE XX

ORDER NO	ITEM NO	UNITS SHIPPED	MESSAGE
999999	99999	999	—
999999	99999	999	—

MITRE-11 HARDWARE
INVENTORY CONTROL
BACK ORDER LIST PAGE XX

ORDER NO	ITEM NO	BACK ORDER QTY
999999	99999	999
999999	99999	999

CHAPTER 8

MODULE DESIGN CONSIDERATIONS

Objectives

- To introduce cohesion as a measure of the internal strength of a module
- To discuss inter-module communication, local and global variables and the passing of parameters between modules
- To introduce coupling as a measure of the extent of information interchange between modules

Outline

8.1 Module cohesion

A *module* has been defined as a section of an algorithm which is dedicated to the performance of a single function. It contains a single entry and a single exit and the name chosen for the module should describe its function.

Beginner programmers often need guidance in determining what makes a *good module*. Common queries are 'How big should a module be?', 'Is this module too small?' or 'Should I put all the read statements in one module?'

There is a method which programmers can use to remove some of the guesswork when establishing modules. The programmer can look at the *cohesion* of the module. Cohesion is a measure of the internal strength of a module, ie how closely the elements or statements of a module are associated with each other. The more closely the elements of a module are associated the higher the cohesion of the module. Modules with high cohesion are considered *good* modules, because of their internal strength.

Edward Yourdon and Larry Constantine[2] established seven levels of cohesion and placed them in a scale from the weakest to the strongest.

Cohesion level	Cohesion attribute	Resultant module strength
Coincidental	Low Cohesion	Weakest
Logical	↓	↓
Temporal		
Procedural		
Communicational		
Sequential		
Functional	High Cohesion	Strongest

Each level of cohesion in the table will be discussed in this chapter and pseudocode examples which illustrate each level will also be provided.

2 Edward Yourdon and Larry Constantine, *Structured Design: Fundamentals of a Discipline of Computer Program and System Design*, Prentice-Hall, 1979

1 Coincidental cohesion

The weakest form of cohesion a module can have is coincidental cohesion. It occurs when elements are formed into a module simply because they happen to fall together. There is no meaningful relationship between the elements at all, and so, it is difficult to concisely define the function of the module.

Fortunately, these types of modules are rare in today's programming practice. They typically used to occur as a result of one of the following conditions:

- An existing program may have been arbitrarily segmented into smaller modules, because of hardware constrictions on the operation of the program.
- Existing modules may have been arbitrarily subdivided to conform to a badly considered programming standard. (For example, each module should have no more than fifty program statements.)
- A number of existing modules may have been combined into one module to either reduce the number of modules in a program or to increase the number of statements in a module to a particular minimum number.

With continually increasing storage capacity and speed of execution, modules which are forced to contain unrelated elements for the above reasons, only rarely occur.

A pseudocode example of a module which has coincidental cohesion follows:

```
File-Processing
   Open employee updates file
   Read employee record
   Print-Page-Headings
   Open employee master file
   Set page-count to one
   Set errors-flag to false
END
```

Notice that the instructions within the module have no meaningful relationship to each other.

2 Logical cohesion

Logical cohesion occurs when the elements of a module are grouped together according to a certain *class* of activity. That is, the elements fall into some general category because they all do the same *kind* of thing.

An example might be a module which performs all the read statements for three different files: a sort of 'Read-all-files' module. To use such a module, the calling module will need to indicate which of the three files it requires the module to read during a particular call.

A module such as this is slightly stronger than a coincidentally cohesive module, because the elements are, at least, somewhat related. However, logically cohesive modules are usually made up of a number of smaller, independent sections, which should exist independently, rather than be combined together because of a related activity. Often when a module such as this is called,only a smallsubset of the elements within the module will be executed.

A pseudocode example for a 'Read-all-files' module might look like this:

```
Read-all-files
   CASE OF file-code
      1 :   Read customer transaction record
            IF not EOF
               increment customer-transaction-count
            ENDIF
      2 :   Read customer master record
            IF not EOF
               increment customer-master-count
            ENDIF
      3 :   Read product master record
            IF not EOF
               increment product-master-count
            ENDIF
   ENDCASE
END
```

Notice that the three read instructions in this module perform three separate functions.

3 Temporal cohesion

Temporal cohesion occurs when the elements of a module are grouped together because they are related by time. Typical examples are initialization and finalization modules, where elements are placed together because they perform certain *housekeeping* functions at the beginning or end of a program.

A temporally cohesive module can be considered a logically cohesive module where *time* is the related activity. However, it is slightly stronger than a logically cohesive module because most of the elements in a time-related module are executed each time the module is called. Usually, however, the elements are not all related to the same function.

A pseudocode example of a temporally cohesive module might look like this:

```
Initialization
   Open Transaction file
   Issue prompt 'Enter todays date — DDMMYY'
   Read todays-date
   Set transaction-count to zero
   Read transaction record
   IF not EOF
      increment transaction-count
   ENDIF
   Open Report file
   Print-Page-Headings
   Set report-total to zero
END
```

Notice that the elements of the module perform a number of functions.

4 Procedural cohesion

Procedural cohesion occurs when the elements of a module are related because they operate according to a particular procedure. That is, the elements are executed in a particular sequence so that the objectives of the program are achieved. As a result, the modules contain elements related more to program procedure than to program function.

A typical example of a procedurally cohesive module is the mainline of a program. The elements of a mainline are grouped together because of a particular procedural order.

The weakness of procedurally cohesive modules is that they cut across functional boundaries. That is, the procedure may contain only part of a function at one level, but at the same time may contain multiple functions at a lower level; as in the pseudocode example below:

```
Read-student-records-and-total-student-ages
   Set number-of-records to zero
   Set total-age to zero
   Read student record
   DOWHILE more records exist
      Add age to total-age
      Add 1 to number-of-records
      Read student record
   ENDDO
END
```

Note that the use of the word 'and' in the module name indicates that this module performs more than one function.

5 Communicational cohesion

Communicational cohesion occurs when the elements of a module are grouped together because they all operate on the same (central) piece of data. Communicationally cohesive modules are commonly found in business applications because of the close relationship of a business program to the data it is processing. For example, a module may contain all the validations of the fields of a record; or all the processing required to assemble a report line for printing.

Communicational cohesion is acceptable because it is data related. It is stronger than procedural cohesion because of its relationship with the data, rather than control-flow sequence.

The weakness of a communicationally cohesive module lies in the fact that usually a combination of processing for a particular piece of data is performed, as in the pseudocode example which follows:

```
Validate-Product-Record
    IF transaction-type NOT = '0' THEN
        errors-flag = true
        error-message = 'invalid transaction type'
        Write-Error-Report
    ENDIF
    IF customer-number is NOT numeric THEN
        errors-flag = true
        error-message = 'invalid customer number'
        Write-Error-Report
    ENDIF
    IF product-no = blanks
    OR product-no has leading blanks THEN
        errors-flag = true
        error-message = 'invalid product no'
        Write-Error-Report
    ENDIF
END
```

6 Sequential cohesion

Sequential cohesion occurs when a module contains elements which are dependent on the processing of previous elements. That is, it might contain elements in which the output data from one element serves as input data to the next. Thus, a sequentially cohesive module is like an assembly line; a series of sequential steps perform successive transformations of data.

Sequential cohesion is stronger than communicational cohesion because it is more problem oriented. Its weakness lies only in the fact that the module may perform multiple functions, or fragments of functions.

A pseudocode example of a sequentially cohesive module follows:

```
Process-Purchases
   Set total-purchases to zero
   Read number-of-purchases
   DO loop-index = 1 to number-of-purchases
      get purchase
      add purchase to total-purchases
   ENDDO
   discount = total-purchases * discount-percent
   amount-due = total-purchases – discount
END
```

Note that this module firstly calculates total-purchases and then uses the variable total-purchases in the subsequent calculation of amount-due.

7 Functional cohesion

Functional cohesion occurs when all the elements of a module contribute to the performance of a single specific task. The module can be easily named by a single verb followed by a two-word object.

Mathematically oriented modules are a good example of functional cohesion, as the elements which make up the module form an integral part of the calculation.

A pseudocode example of a functionally cohesive module is the module 'Calculate-Discount':

```
Calculate-Discount
   IF product is rated zero discount THEN
      discount = 0
   ELSE
      IF product-price < £50.00 THEN
         discount = product price * 0.25
      ELSE
         IF product-price < £100.00 THEN
            discount = product-price * 0.35
         ELSE
            discount = product-price * 0.5
         ENDIF
      ENDIF
   ENDIF
END
```

8 A summary of cohesion levels

When designing a program's structure the programmer should try to form modules which have a single problem-related function. If functional cohesion is achieved, then the modules will be more independent; easier to read and understand; and more maintainable than modules with lesser cohesion.

In some cases, it is not always easy to construct a program where *every* module has functional cohesion. Some modules may contain lower levels of cohesion, or even a combination of types of cohesion. This may not be a problem. However, it is important that the programmer is able to recognize the various cohesion levels and is able to justify a module with a lower cohesion in a particular set of circumstances.

The prime consideration a programmer must make is to produce modules and programs which are easy to understand and modify. The higher the cohesion of the modules, the more likely the programmer has achieved this aim.

8.2 Inter-module communication

When designing modular programs a programmer should consider not only the cohesion of the module, but the flow of information between the modules. The fewer and simpler the communications between modules, the easier it is to understand and maintain one module without reference to other modules.

Inter-module communication can be accomplished by using:

1 global data, or
2 a list of parameters.

Global data

In all our examples information or. data has been passed from one module to another, by using the same variable names in both the calling module and the called modules of a program. This data is known as *global data*, as it is known to the *whole world* of the program. The data can be accessed by every module in the program. Thus, it can be said that the *scope* of a global variable is the whole program. (The scope of a variable is a list of all the modules in which it could be referenced.)

All data, however, does not need to be global.

Local data

Variables which are defined within a subordinate module are called *local variables*. These local variables are not known to the calling module, or any other module. The *scope* of a local variable then is simply the module in which it is defined.

Using local variables can reduce what is known as program *side effects*.

Side effects

A *side effect* is a form of cross-communication of a module with other parts of a program. It occurs when a subordinate module alters the value of a global variable inside a module. Side effects are not necessarily detrimental. However, they do tend to decrease the manageability of a program and a programmer should be aware of their impact.

If a program is amended at any time by a programmer other than the person who wrote it, a change may be made to a global variable. This change could cause *side effects* or erroneous results because the maintenance programmer is unaware of other modules which also alter that global variable.

Passing parameters

Another method of inter-module communication is the passing of *parameters* or *arguments* between modules. A parameter can be a variable, literal or constant which can communicate between various parts of a program.

A parameter may have one of three functions:

1 The parameter may be used to pass information from a calling module to a subordinate module. The subordinate module would then use that information in its processing, but would not need to communicate any information back to the calling module.

2 The parameter may be used to pass information from a subordinate module to its calling module. The calling module would then use that parameter in subsequent processing.

3 The parameter may be used to fulfill a two-way communication role. Information may be passed by the calling module to a subordinate module, where it is amended in some fashion and then passed back to the calling module.

These parameters which pass between modules can be incorporated into a hierarchy chart or structure chart using the following symbols:

for data parameters

for status parameters

Data parameters contain the actual variables or data items which will be passed between modules.

Status parameters act as program *flags* and should contain just one of two values: true or false. These program flags or switches are set to *true* or *false,* according to a specific set of conditions. They are then used to control further processing.

When designing modular programs, the programmer should avoid using data parameters to also indicate status. This can affect the program in two ways:

1 It may confuse the reader of the program because a variable has been *overloaded;* ie it has been used for more than one purpose; and
2 It may cause unpredictable errors when the program is amended at some later date as the maintenance programmer may be unaware of the dual purpose of the variable.

8.3 Using parameters in program design

Let us look at an example which uses parameters in its module design. (The program could also have been developed using global data variables.)

Example 8.1 Process three numbers

Design a program which will prompt for and *read* three numbers from the screen, *sort* them into ascending order and *print* them, in sorted order, onto the screen.

a Define the problem

INPUT	*PROCESSING*	*OUTPUT*
Num1	Read three numbers	Num1
Num2	Sort three numbers	Num2
Num3	Print sorted numbers	Num3

b Group the activities into modules

The activities can be grouped into three main functions:

1 Read-Three-Numbers
2 Sort-Three-Numbers
3 Print-Sorted-Numbers

The module 'Sort-Three-Numbers' will call on another module named 'Order-Two-Numbers'. This module will place any two numbers passed to it, into ascending sequence. By calling 'Order-Two-Numbers' three times, each with a different pair of numbers passed to it, the three numbers will be successfully sorted.

c Construct a hierarchy chart

The hierarchy chart will show not only the modules and their relationship to each other, but also the parameters which are to be passed between the modules.

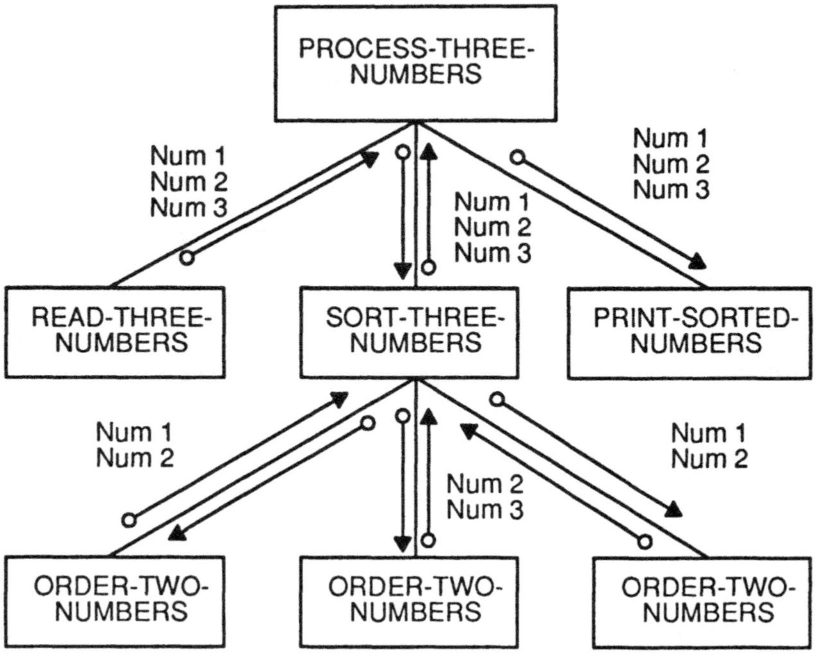

d Establish the logic of the mainline of the algorithm using pseudocode

The mainline will require calls to each of the three subordinate modules.

1 'Read-Three-Numbers' will return three numbers to the mainline.
2 'Sort-Three-Numbers' will have three numbers passed to it, when it is called. It will then make adjustments to the three numbers, using a module 'Order-Two-Numbers' and pass the three numbers, in sorted order, back to the mainline.
3 'Print-Sorted-Numbers' will have the three sorted numbers passed to it when it is called.

Parameters are represented in pseudocode as variables within curved brackets. The mainline of this program will then simply list the calls to its subordinate modules and the parameters it passes.

```
Process-Three-Numbers
   Read-Three-Numbers (Num1, Num2, Num3)
   Sort-Three-Numbers (Num1, Num2, Num3)
   Print-Sorted-Numbers (Num1, Num2, Num3)
END
```

e Establish the pseudocode for each successive module in the hierarchy chart

1 'Read-Three-Numbers' is a simple module which will prompt for and read three numbers.

```
Read-Three-Numbers (Num1, Num2, Num3)
   Write 'Enter three real numbers'
   Read Num1
   Read Num2
   Read Num3
END
```

2 'Sort-Three-Numbers' will call 'Order-Two-Numbers' three times, each time passing a different pair of numbers. Different values may be placed into Num1, Num2 and Num3 as a result of each call.

```
Sort-Three-Numbers (Num1, Num2, Num3)
   Order-Two-Numbers (Num1, Num2)
   Order-Two-Numbers (Num2, Num3)
   Order-Two-Numbers (Num1, Num2)
END
```

3 'Print-Sorted-Numbers' will have the three sorted numbers passed to it when it is called.

```
Print-Sorted-Numbers (Num1, Num2, Num3)
   Write 'The three numbers in sorted order are'
   Write Num1, Num2, Num3
END
```

4 The module 'Order-Two-Numbers' uses a local variable 'Tempnum' which will *hold* a value during the interchange process, if required. Different values will be provided for the parameters Num1 and Num2 each time the module is called.

```
Order-Two-Numbers (Num1, Num2)
   IF Num1 > Num2 THEN
      Tempnum = Num1
      Num1 = Num2
      Num2 = Tempnum
   ENDIF
END
```

f Desk check the solution algorithm

(i) Input Data:

Two test cases with the three numbers in different order should be sufficient to desk check the algorithm.

	First Data Set	Second Data Set
Num1	10.3	17.8
Num2	18.5	16.3
Num3	12.6	15.1

(ii) Expected Result:

The three numbers in sorted order are

10.3	12.6	18.5
15.1	16.3	17.8

(iii) Desk Check Table:

Statements	Num1	Num2	Num3	Tempnum
Read-Three-Numbers	10.3	18.5	12.6	
Sort-Three-Numbers				
Order-Two-Numbers	10.3	18.5		
Order-Two-Numbers		12.6	18.5	18.5
Order-Two-Numbers	10.3	12.6		
Print-Sorted-Numbers	10.3	12.6	18.5	
Read-Three-Numbers	17.8	16.3	15.1	
Sort-Three-Numbers				
Order-Two-Numbers	16.3	17.8		17.8
Order-Two-Numbers		15.1	17.8	17.8
Order-Two-Numbers	15.1	16.3		16.3
Print-Sorted-Numbers	15.1	16.3	17.8	

8.4 Module coupling

When designing a solution algorithm, a programmer should look not only at the cohesion of the modules, but also the flow of information between modules.

The programmer should aim towards module independence. That is, towards modules which have fewer and simpler connections with other modules. The fewer these connections, then the easier it is to maintain one module without reference to other modules. These connections are called *interfaces* or *couples*.

Coupling is a measure of the extent of information interchange between modules. Tight coupling implies large dependence on the structure of one module by another. Because there are a higher number of connections, there are many paths along which errors can extend into other parts of the program.

Loose coupling is the opposite of tight coupling. Modules with loose coupling are more independent and easier to maintain.

Glenford Myers[2] devised a coupling scale, similar to Yourdon and Constantine's cohesion scale.

Coupling Level	Coupling Attribute	Resultant Module Design Quality
Common	Tight coupling	poorest
External	↓	↓
Control		
Stamp		
Data	Loose coupling	best

The five levels of coupling are listed in a scale from the poorest module design quality to the best. Each of the levels of coupling will be discussed and pseudocode examples which illustrate each level will be provided. It should be noted that these levels of coupling are not definitive. They are merely those coupling levels which Glenford Myers believes can exist in modular programs.

1 Common coupling

Common coupling occurs when modules reference the same global *data structure*. (A data structure is a collection of related fields, such as a

2 Glenford Myers, *Composite Structured Design*, Van Nostrand Reinhold, 1978

record, or an array.) When data is common coupled, it is shared by the modules.

This means the data can be accessed and modified by any module in the program. This can make the program difficult to read.

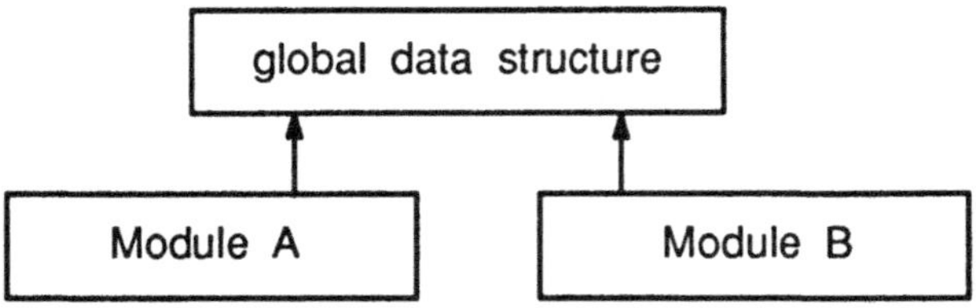

A pseudocode example of two modules which are common coupled follows:

```
A Read-Customer-Record
      Read customer record
      IF EOF THEN
         set EOF-flag to true
      ENDIF
  END

B Validate-Customer-Record
      IF customer-number is NOT numeric THEN
         error-message = 'invalid customer number'
         Write-Error-Report
      ENDIF
      :
      :
  END
```

Both modules access the same global data structure: 'customer-record'.

2 External coupling

External coupling occurs when two or more modules access the same global data *variable*.

It is similar to common coupling. The difference is that the global data is a variable, rather than a data structure. Because of this, external coupling is considered to be looser than common coupling.

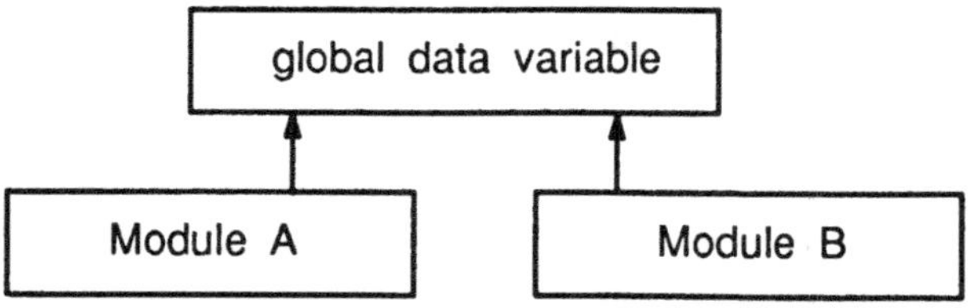

A pseudocode example of two modules which exhibit external coupling follows:

```
A Calculate-Discount
    IF product is rated zero discount THEN
      discount = 0
    ELSE
      IF product-price < £50.00 THEN
        discount = product price * 0.25
      .
      .
      .
      ENDIF
    ENDIF
  END

B Calculate-Amount-Due
    .
    .
    .
    .
    Amount-due = Total-amount - discount
  END
```

Both modules access the same global data variable 'discount'.

3 Control coupling

Control coupling occurs when a module passes a control variable to another module, which is intended to control the other module's logic. These control variables are referred to as program flags, or switches and are passed between modules in the form of parameters.

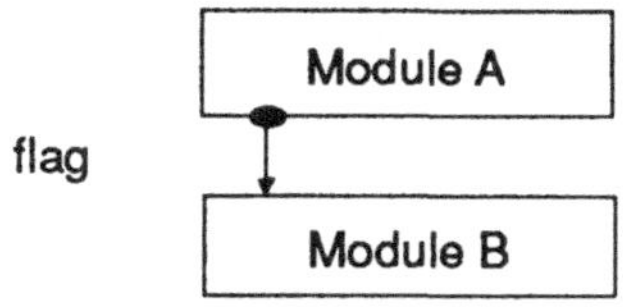

The weakness of control coupled modules is that the passing of the control field between modules implies that one module is aware of the internal logic of the other. Often this type of coupling indicates that the subordinate module is logically cohesive, as follows:

```
A Process-Input-Code
      Read Input-Code
      Choice (input-code)
      .
      .
      .
      .
  END

B Choice (input-code)
      CASE OF input-code
         1 : Read employee record
         2 : Print-Page-Headings
         3 : Open employee master file
         4 : Set page-count to zero
         5 : Error-message = 'Employee number not numeric'
      ENDCASE
  END
```

The control field in this example is the parameter 'input-code'.

4 Stamp coupling

Stamp coupling occurs when one module passes a non-global data *structure* to another module. The non-global data structure is passed in the form of a parameter.

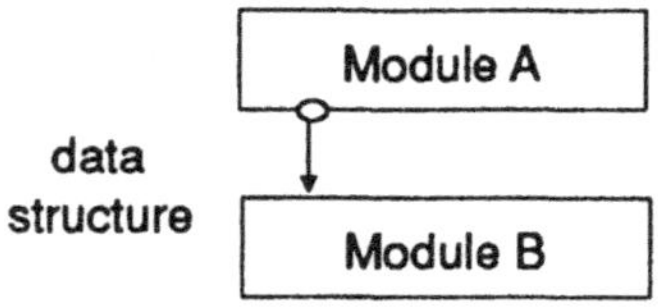

Stamp coupled modules demonstrate loose coupling and offer good module design quality. The only relationship between the two modules is the passing of the data structure between them; there is no need for either module to know the internal logic of the other.

A pseudocode example of two stamp coupled modules follows:

```
A Process-Transaction-Record
      .
      .
      .
      .
      IF transaction record is for a male THEN
         Process-Male-Student (Current-record)
      ELSE
         Process-Female-Student (Current-record)
      ENDIF
      .
      .
      .
      .
   END

B Process-Male-Student (Current-record)
      Increment male-student-count
      IF student-age > 21 THEN
         increment mature-male-count
      ENDIF
      .
      .
      .
      .
   END
```

The only relationship between the two modules is the passing of the data structure 'Current-record'.

5 Data coupling

Data coupling occurs when a module passes a non-global data *variable* to another module. It is similar to stamp coupling. The difference is that the non-global data item is a variable, not a data structure.

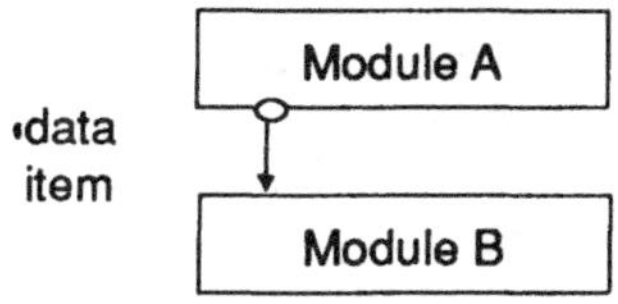

Modules which are data coupled demonstrate the loosest coupling and offer the best module design qualities. The only relationship between the two modules is the passing of the data item(s) between them.

A pseudocode example of two data coupled modules follows:

```
A Process-Customer-Record
      .
      .
      .
      Calculate-Discount (total price, discount)
      .
      .
      .
      .
      .
  END

B Calculate-Discount (total-price, discount)
      IF total-price < £10.00 THEN
         discount = total-price * 0.25
      ELSE
         IF total-price < £100.00 THEN
            discount = total-price * 0.3
         ELSE
            discount = total-price * 0.4
         ENDIF
      ENDIF
  END
```

In this example, the only connection between the two modules is the passing of the variables 'total-price' and 'discount' between them.

6 A summary of coupling levels

When designing solution algorithms, the programmer should aim towards module independence and a minimum of information interchange between modules.

The programmer should aim at *uncoupling* each module from its surroundings by:

1 Passing data to a subordinate module in the form of parameters, rather than using global data, and
2 Writing each subordinate module as a self-contained unit which can accept data passed to it; operate on it without reference to other parts of the program; and pass information back to the calling module, if required.

However, the prime consideration a programmer must have is to produce modules and programs which are easily understood and modified. If the chosen programming language only offers global data, then the fact that the program has been well designed will minimize the effects of tight coupling.

8.5 Chapter summary

This chapter covered a number of different topics which a programmer should consider when designing modular programs. A program which has been well designed has modules which are independent, easy to read and easily maintained. Such modules are likely to exhibit high cohesion and loose coupling.

Cohesion is a measure of the internal strength of a module. The higher the cohesion, the better the module. Seven levels of cohesion were given and each level was discussed, with a pseudocode example provided.

Coupling is a measure of the extent of information interchange between modules. The fewer the connections between modules, the more loosely they are coupled, offering good module design quality. Five levels of coupling were given and each level was discussed, with a pseudocode example provided.

Inter-module communication was defined as the flow of information or data between modules. Local and global variables were introduced, along with the *scope* of a variable and the *side effect* of using only global data.

Parameters were introduced as another method of inter-module communication. A method of representing parameters on a structure chart was devised and a programming example which used parameters was developed.

8.6 Programming problems

Construct a solution algorithm for the following programming problems. Each solution algorithm should be designed so that parameters are passed between modules to provide greater module independence. If possible, each module should demonstrate high cohesion and loose coupling.

To obtain your final solution you should:

- define the problem
- group the activities into modules (also consider the data which each module requires)
- construct a hierarchy chart
- establish the logic of the mainline using pseudocode

- develop the pseudocode for each successive module in the hierarchy chart, and
- desk check the solution algorithm.

1 Design a program which will prompt for and read five numbers from the screen, calculate the sum and the average of the numbers and print these calculated values onto the screen.

2 Design a program which will prompt for and read a four digit representation of the year. The program is to determine if the year provided is a leap year and to print a message to this effect on the screen. A message is also to be printed on the screen if the value provided is not exactly four numeric digits.

3 Design a program which will read a file of sales volume records and print a report showing the sales commission owing to each salesperson.

Each input record contains salesperson number, name and their volume of sales for the month.

The commission rate varies according to sales volume as follows:

On sales volume up to (£)	*Commission rate (%)*
200	5
1000	8
2000	10
4000 and above	12

The calculated commission may be a combination of amounts according to the sales volume figure. For example, the commission owing for a sales volume of £1200 would be calculated as follows:

Commission=(200 * 5%)+((1000 – 200) * 8%)+((1200 – 1000) * 10%)

Your program is to print the salesperson number, name, their volume of sales and their calculated commission, with the appropriate column headings.

CHAPTER 9

GENERAL PSEUDOCODE ALGORITHMS TO COMMON BUSINESS PROBLEMS

Objective

- To provide general pseudocode algorithms to five common business applications. Topics covered are:
  - — report generation with page break
  - — single-level control break
  - — multiple-level control break
  - — sequential file update
  - — array processing

Outline

9.1 Program structure
9.2 Report generation with page break
9.3 Single-level control break
9.4 Multiple-level control break
9.5 Sequential file update
9.6 Array processing
9.7 Chapter summary
9.8 Programming problems

9.1 Program structure

The aim of this chapter is to present a number of general pseudocode solutions to a selection of typical programming problems. All of the features covered in the previous eight chapters have been incorporated into these solutions, with the result that each solution offers a sound modular structure with highly cohesive modules.

For ease of presentation, the solutions have been designed to use global data. They could, however, easily be adjusted to incorporate the passing of parameters as in the example in Chapter 8.

Throughout this text, reference has been made to a general solution algorithm for the processing of sequential files. This algorithm is a *skeleton solution* and in pseudocode, looks like this:

```
Process-Sequential-File
    DO Initial Processing
    Read first record
    DOWHILE more records exist
        Process this record
        Read next record
    ENDDO
    DO Final Processing
END
```

This basic solution algorithm forms the framework for almost all commercial business programs. It does not include processing for page headings, control breaks, total lines or special calculations. However, the programmer can easily incorporate these requirements by expanding this general solution.

This general solution algorithm can also be modularized:

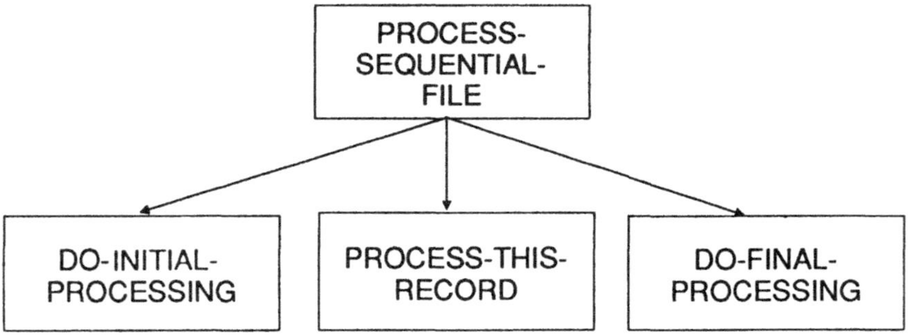

```
Process-Sequential-File
   Do-Initial-Processing
   Read first record
   DOWHILE more records exist
      Process-This-Record
      Read next record
   ENDDO
   Do-Final-Processing
END
```

The module 'Process-This-Record' can be extended, as required, for the processing of a particular programming problem. Let us now use this basic program structure to develop solution algorithms to five common business programming applications.

9.2 Report generation with page break

Most reports require page heading lines, column heading lines, detail lines, and total lines. Reports are also required to skip to a new page after a pre-determined number of detail lines have been printed.

A typical report might look like this:

	GLAD RAGS CLOTHING COMPANY		
12/05/89	CURRENT ACCOUNT BALANCES		PAGE: 1
CUSTOMER NUMBER	CUSTOMER NAME	CUSTOMER ADDRESS	ACCOUNT BALANCE
12345	SPORTY'S	THE MALL, REDFERN	300.50
12346	SLINKY'S	PICNIC RD, PYMBLE	400.50
	TOTAL CUSTOMERS ON FILE		200
	TOTAL CUSTOMERS WITH BALANCE OWING		150
	TOTAL BALANCE OWING		4 300.00

Our general solution algorithm for processing a sequential file can be extended by the addition of new modules which cater for these report requirements, as follows:

a Hierarchy chart

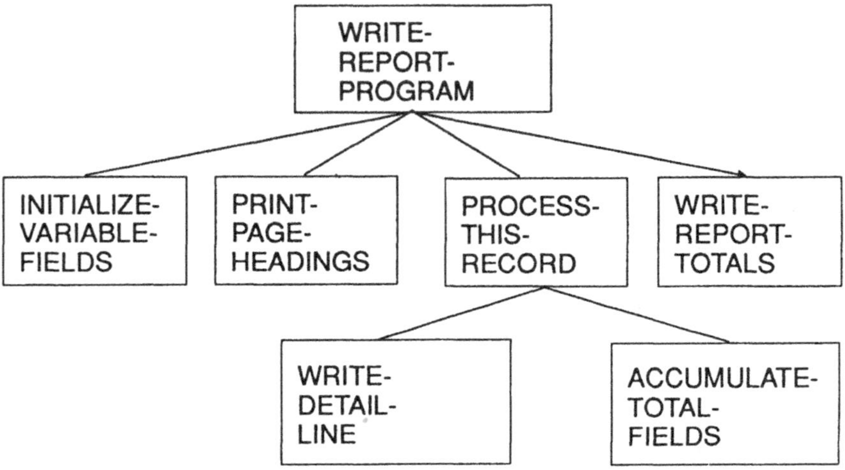

Once the hierarchy chart has been established, the solution algorithm can be developed in pseudocode.

b Solution algorithm

Mainline

```
Write-Report-Program
   Initialize-Variable-Fields
   Print-Page-Headings
   Read first record
   DOWHILE more records exist
      IF line count > max-detail-lines THEN
         Print-Page-Headings
         set linecount to zero
      ENDIF
      Process-This-Record
      Read next record
   ENDDO
   Write-Report-Totals
END
```

Subordinate modules

```
1  Initialize-Variable-Fields
      set accumulators to zero
      set pagecount to zero
      set linecount to zero
      set max-detail-lines to designated value
   END

2  Print-Page-Headings
      increment pagecount
      write heading lines
      write column heading lines
      write blank line (if required)
   END

3  Process-This-Record
      do necessary calculations (if any)
      Write-Detail-Line
      Accumulate-Total-Fields
   END

4  Write-Report-Totals
      build total line(s)
      write total line(s)
   END

5  Write-Detail-Line
      build detail line
      write detail line
      increment linecount
   END

6  Accumulate-Total-Fields
      increment accumulators as required
   END
```

This general pseudocode solution can now be used as a framework for any report program which requires page breaks.

9.3 Single-level control break

Printed reports, which also produce control break total lines are very common in business applications. A control break total line is a summary line for a group of records which contain the same record *key*. This record *key* is a designated field on each record, and is referred to as the control field. The *control field* is used to identify a record or a group of records within a file. A control break occurs each time there is a change in value of the control field. Thus, control break total lines are printed each time a control break is detected.

Reports which print control break totals can be categorized as being either single-level or multiple-level control break reports depending on whether there is one control field or more than one control field respectively.

Let us look at a single-level control break report.

MULTI-DISK COMPUTER COMPANY

12/05/89 SALES REPORT BY SALESPERSON PAGE: 1

SALESPERSON NUMBER	SALESPERSON NAME	PRODUCT NUMBER	QTY SOLD	PRICE	EXTENSION AMOUNT
1001	MARY SMITH	1032	2	10.00	20.00
		1033	2	20.00	40.00
		1044	2	30.00	60.00
		SALES TOTAL FOR MARY SMITH			120.00
1002	JANE BROWN	1032	2	10.00	20.00
		1045	1	35.00	35.00
		SALES TOTAL FOR JANE BROWN			55.00
		REPORT SALES TOTAL			175.00

Note that a control break total line is printed, each time the salesperson number changes.

There are two considerations that a programmer must take into account when designing a control break program:

1 The file to be processed must have been sorted into control field sequence. (In the example above the file was sorted into ascending sequence of salesperson number). If the file has not been sorted, then erroneous results will occur.
2 Each time a record is read from the input file, the control field on the current record must be compared with the control field on the record just printed. If the control fields are different, then a control break total line must be printed for the record just completed.

The general solution algorithm which was developed for a Report Generation program can be extended by the addition of two new modules to incorporate a single-level control break. These modules are named 'Write-Control-Total-Line', and 'Reset-Control-Totals'.

a Hierarchy chart

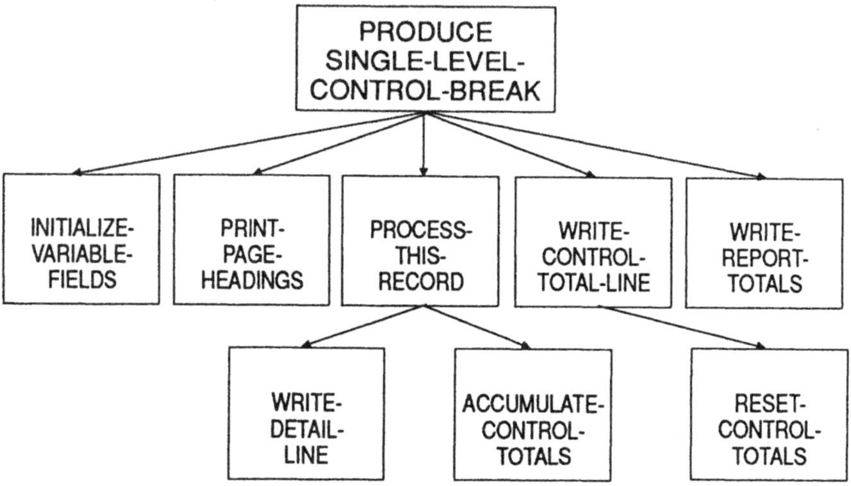

All control break report programs will require the following variables:

1 A variable named 'this-control-field' which will hold the control field of the record just read.
2 A variable named 'previous-control-field' which will hold the control field of the previous record. The variable 'previous-control-field' will be set to the same value as 'this-control-field' to cater for the processing of the first record.
3 A variable, or variables, to accumulate the control break totals.
4 A variable to accumulate the report totals.

b Solution algorithm

Mainline

```
Produce-Single-Level-Control-Break
    Initialize-Variable-Fields
    Print-Page-Headings
    Read first record
    this-control-field = control field
    previous-control-field = control field
    DOWHILE more records exist
        IF this-control-field NOT = previous-control-field THEN
            Write-Control-Total-Line
```

```
        previous-control-field = this-control-field
    ENDIF
    IF linecount  > max-detail-lines THEN
        Print-Page-Headings
        set linecount to zero
    ENDIF
    Process-This-Record
    Read next record
    this-control-field = control field
  ENDDO
  Write-Control-Total-Line
  Write-Report-Totals
END
```

There are four points which should be noted in this mainline algorithm which are essential for a control break program to function correctly.

1 Each time a new record is read from the file, the new control field is assigned to the variable 'this-control-field'.
2 When the first record is read the new control field is assigned to both the variables 'this-control-field' and 'previous-control-field'. This will prevent the control totals printing before the first record has been processed.
3 The variable 'previous-control-field' is updated as soon as a change in the control field is detected.
4 After the end of the file has been detected, the module 'Write-Control-Total-Line' is called. This will then print the control break totals for the last record or set of records.

Subordinate modules

```
1 Initialize-Variable-Fields
    set control total accumulators to zero
    set report total accumulators to zero
    set pagecount to zero
    set linecount to zero
    set max-detail-lines to designated value
  END

2 Print-Page-Headings
    increment pagecount
    write heading lines
    write column heading lines
    write blank line (if required)
  END
```

```
3 Process-This-Record
     do necessary calculations (if any)
     Write-Detail-Line
     Accumulate-Control-Totals
  END

4 Write-Control-Total-Line
     build control total line
     write control total line
     write blank line (if required)
     increment linecount
     Reset-Control-Totals
  END

5 Write-Report-Totals
     build report total line
     write report total line
  END

6 Write-Detail-Line
     build detail line
     write detail line
     increment linecount
  END

7 Accumulate-Control-Totals
     increment control total accumulators
  END

8 Reset-Control-Totals
     add control total accumulators to report total accumulators
     set control total accumulators to zero
  END
```

Notice that when a control total line is printed, the module 'Reset-Control-Totals' is called. This module will add the control totals to the report totals and reset the control totals to zero for the next set of records. This general solution algorithm can now be used as a framework for any single-level control break program.

9.4 Multiple-level control break

Algorithms to print reports which produce single-level control break totals have already been covered. Often, however, reports are required to include multiple-level control break totals. For instance, the Sales Report produced in section 9.3 may require sales totals for each salesperson in the company, and also, sales totals for each department within the company.

The Monthly Sales Report might then look like this:

```
                     MULTI-DISK COMPUTER COMPANY
12/05/89                      SALES REPORT                      PAGE: 1
DEPT   SALESPERSON  SALESPERSON   PRODUCT  QTY    PRICE  EXTENSION
       NUMBER       NAME          NUMBER   SOLD          AMOUNT

01     1001         MARY SMITH    1032     2      10.00   20.00
                                  1033     2      20.00   40.00
                                  1044     2      30.00   60.00
                         SALES TOTAL FOR MARY SMITH      120.00

       1002         JANE BROWN    1032     2      10.00   20.00
                                  1045     1      35.00   35.00
                         SALES TOTAL FOR JANE BROWN       55.00
                         SALES TOTAL FOR DEPT 01         175.00

02     1050         JENNY PONDS   1033     2      20.00   40.00
                                  1044     2      30.00   60.00
                         SALES TOTAL FOR JENNY PONDS     100.00
                         SALES TOTAL FOR DEPT 02         100.00

                         REPORT SALES TOTAL              275.00
```

Note that a control break total line is printed each time the salesperson number changes, and each time the department number changes. Thus, there are two control fields in this file.

The same concepts which applied to a single-level control break program, also apply to a multiple-level control break program:

1 The input file must be sorted into control field sequence. When there is more than one control field, the file must be sorted into sequence of minor control field within major control field. (To

produce the Sales Report, the Sales File must have been sorted into salesperson-number within department-number.)

2 Each time a record is read from the file, the control fields on the current record must be compared with the control fields of the record just printed. If the minor control fields have changed, then the control totals for the previous minor control field must be printed. If the major control fields have changed, then the control fields for the previous major control field and minor control field must be printed.

The general solution algorithm which was developed for a single-level control break program can be extended by the addition of two new modules to incorporate a two-level control break. If three control breaks were required, then another two modules would be added to the solution algorithm, and so on.

The names of the modules which produce the control totals have been changed slightly, so that they indicate which level of control break has occurred. These new module names are: 'Write-Minor-Control-Totals' 'Write-Major-Control-Totals', 'Reset-Minor-Control-Totals' and 'Reset-Major-Control-Totals'.

a Hierarchy chart

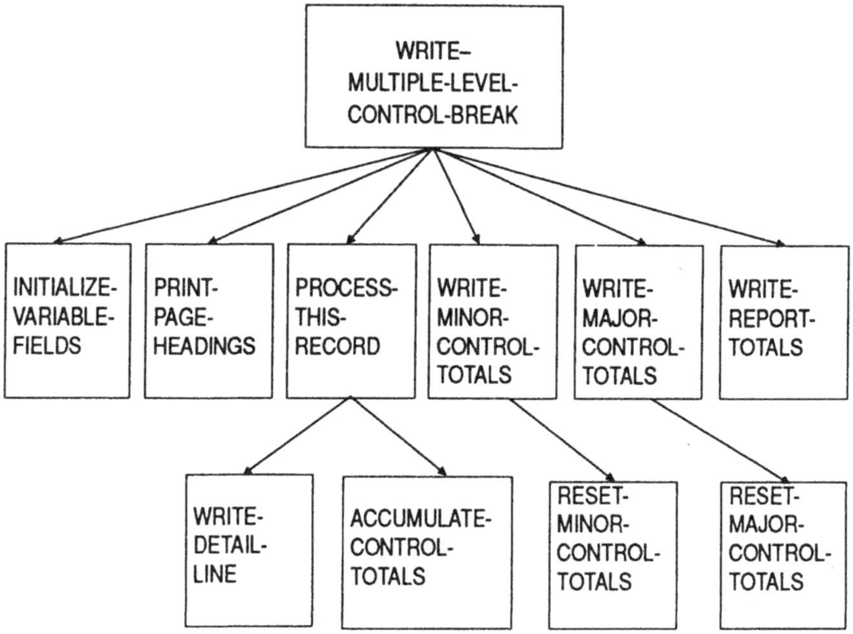

b Solution algorithm

Mainline

```
Produce-Multiple-Level-Control-Break
    Initialize-Variable-Fields
    Print-Page-Headings
    Read first record
    this-minor-control-field = previous-minor-control-field = minor control field
    this-major-control-field = previous-major-control-field = major control field
    DOWHILE more records exist
        IF this-major-control-field NOT = previous-major-control-field THEN
            Write-Minor-Control-Totals
            previous-minor-control-field = this-minor-control-field
            Write-Major-Control-Totals
            previous-major-control-field = this-major-control-field
        ELSE
            IF this-minor-control-field NOT = previous-minor-control-field THEN
                Write-Minor-Control-Totals
                previous-minor-control-field = this-minor-control-field
            ENDIF
        ENDIF
        IF linecount > max-detail-lines THEN
            Print-Page-Headings
            set linecount to zero
        ENDIF
        Process-This-Record
        Read next record
        this-minor-control-field = minor control field
        this-major-control-field = major control field
    ENDDO
    Write-Minor-Control-Totals
    Write-Major-Control-Totals
    Write-Report-Totals
END
```

The points to be noted in this mainline are:

1 Each time a new record is read from the input file, the new control fields are assigned to the variables 'this-minor-control-field' and 'this-major-control-field'.
2 When the first record is read, the new control fields are assigned to both the current and previous control field variables. This will prevent control totals printing before the first record has been processed.
3 After the end of the input file has been detected, the two modules 'Write-Minor-Control-Totals' and 'Write-Major-Control-Totals' will be called. This will then print control totals for the last minor

control field record, or set of records, and the last major control field set of records.

Subordinate modules

```
1  Initialize-Variable-Fields
       set minor control total accumulators to zero
       set major control total accumulators to zero
       set report total accumulators to zero
       set pagecount to zero
       set linecount to zero
       set max-detail-lines to designated value
   END


2  Print-Page-Headings
       increment page counter
       write heading lines
       write column heading lines
       write blank line (if required)
   END


3  Process-This-Record
       do necessary calculations (if any)
       Write-Detail-Line
       Accumulate-Control-Totals
   END


4  Write-Minor-Control-Totals
       build minor control total line
       write minor control total line
       write blank line (if required)
       increment linecount
       Reset-Minor-Control-Totals
   END


5  Write-Major-Control-Totals
       build major control total line
       write major control total line
       write blank line (if required)
       increment linecount
       Reset-Major-Control-Totals
   END
```

```
6 Write-Report-Totals
     build report total line
     write report total line
  END

7 Write-Detail-Line
     build detail line
     write detail line
     increment linecount
  END

8 Accumulate-Control-Totals
     increment minor control total accumulators
  END

9 Reset-Minor-Control-Totals
     add minor control total accumulators to major control
        total accumulators
     set minor control total accumulators to zero
  END

10 Reset-Major-Control-Totals
     add major control total accumulators to report total accumulators
     set major control total accumulators to zero
  END
```

Because the solution algorithm has simple design, and good modular structure, the processing of intermediate control field breaks as well as major and minor control field breaks can be handled easily. The solution algorithm would simply require the addition of two new modules: 'Write-Intermediate-Control-Totals' and 'Reset-Intermediate-Control-Totals'. The IF statement in the mainline would then be expanded to include this extra condition, as follows:

```
IF this-major-control-field NOT = previous-major-control-field THEN
   Write-Minor-Control-Totals
   previous-minor-control-field = this-minor-control-field
   Write-Intermediate-Control-Totals
   previous-intermediate-control-field = this-intermediate-control-field
   Write-Major-Control-Totals
   previous-major-control-field = this-major-control-field
ELSE
   IF this-intermediate-control-field NOT = previous-intermediate-
   control-field THEN
      Write-Minor-Control-Totals
      previous-minor-control-field = this-minor-control-field
      Write-Intermediate-Control-Totals
      previous-intermediate-control-field = this-intermediate-control-field
   ELSE
      IF this-minor-control-field NOT = previous-minor-control field  THEN
         Write-Minor-Control-Totals
         previous-minor-control-field = this-minor-control-field
      ENDIF
   ENDIF
ENDIF
```

This pseudocode algorithm can now be used to process any multiple-level control break program.

9.5 Sequential file update

Sequential file updating is a very common batch processing application. It involves the updating of a master file by the application of update transactions on a transaction file. Both files are sequential. A new master file, which incorporates the update transactions is produced. Usually audit reports and error reports are also printed.

A system flow chart of a sequential update program would look like this:

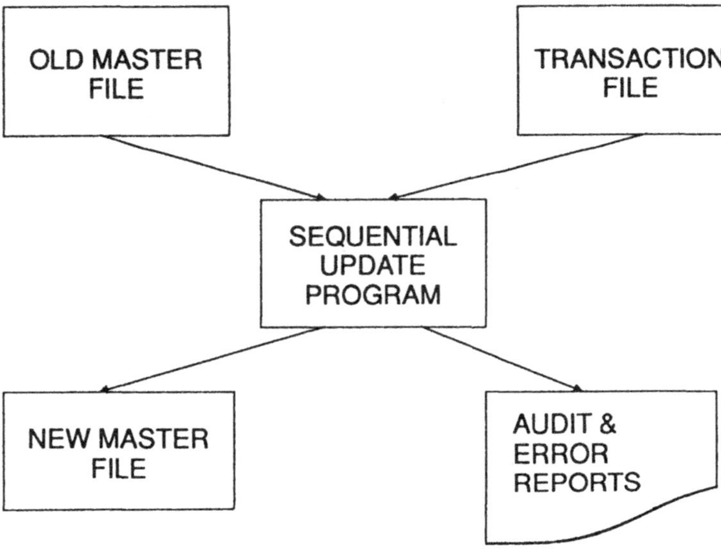

System concepts

1 Master file

A master file is a file which contains permanent and semi-permanent information about the data entities that are contained within it. The records on the master file are in sequence, according to a key field (or fields) on each record. For example, a customer master file may contain the customer's name, address, phone number, credit rating and current balance.

2 Transaction file

A transaction file contains all the data and activities which are not included on the master file. If the transaction file has been designed specifically to update a master file, then there are usually three types of update transactions on this file. These are transactions to:

- add a new record,
- update or change an existing record, and
- delete an existing record.

For example, a customer transaction file might contain transactions which are intended to add a new customer record, change some data on an existing customer record, or delete a customer record on the customer master file. The transaction file is also in sequence according to the same key field as the master record.

3 Audit report

An audit report is a detailed list of all the transactions which were applied to the master file. It provides an accounting trail of the update activities which take place and is used for control purposes.

4 Error report

An error report is a detailed list of any errors which occurred during the processing of the update. Typical errors might be the attempted update of a record which is not on the master file, or the addition of a record which already exists. This error report will require some action to confirm and correct the identified errors.

Sequential update logic

The logic of a sequential update program is more difficult than the other problems encountered, because there are two sequential input files. Processing involves reading a record from each of the input files, and comparing the keys of the two records. As a result of this comparison, processing falls, generally, into three categories:

1 If the transaction record key is less than the old master record key, then the transaction is probably an *add* transaction. The details on the transaction record should then be put into master record format, and the record should be written to the new master file. Another record should then be read from the transaction file.

2 If the transaction record key is equal to the old master record key, then the transaction is probably an *update* or *delete* transaction. If the transaction is an update, then the master record should be amended to reflect the required changes. If the transaction is a delete, then the master record should be flagged as deleted, and should not be written to the new master file. Another transaction record should then be read from the transaction file.

3 If the transaction record key is greater than the old master record key, then there is no matching transaction for that master record. In this case the old master record should be written *unchanged* to the new master file and another record read from the old master file.

Sequential update programs also need to include logic which will handle multiple transaction records for the same master record, and the possibility of transaction records which are in error. The types of transaction record errors which can occur are:

1 An attempt to add a new master record, but a record with that key already exists on the master file.

2 An attempt to update a master record, but there is no record on the master file with that key.
3 An attempt to delete a master record but there is no record on the master file with that key.

Balance line algorithm

The logic of the sequential update program has fascinated programmers for many years. Textbook authors have offered many and varied solutions to solving the problem, but none of these have been a truly *general* solution. Most solutions have been designed around a specific programming language.

A good general solution algorithm written in pseudocode was presented by Barry Dwyer in a paper titled *One More Time — How to Update a Master File.*[1] This algorithm has been referred to as the *balance line algorithm.* It handles multiple transaction records for the one master record, and the possibility of transaction record errors.

A modularized version of the balance line algorithm will be presented in this chapter. It introduces the concept of a *current record.* The current record is the record which is currently being processed, ready for updating and writing to the new master file. The current record is established when the record keys on the two files are compared. The current record will be the record which has the smaller record key. Its format will be that of a new master record. Thus, if the transaction record key is less than the old master record key, the current record will be made up of the fields on the transaction record. If the transaction record key equals the old master record key, or is greater than the old master record key, then the old master record will become the current record.

The current record will remain the current record until there are no more transactions to be applied to that record. It will then be written to the new master file, and a new current record will be established.

Another variable, named *current-record-status* is used as a program flag to indicate whether or not the current record is available for processing. If the current-record-status is *active* then this indicates that the current record has been established and is available for updating, or writing out to the new master file. If the current-record-status is *inactive,* then this indicates that the current record is not available to be updated, or written to the new master file, eg the current record may have been marked for deletion.

1 B Dwyer, '*One More Time – How to Update a Master File*', *Communications of the ACM*, Vol 124, No 1, January 1981

The processing of the two files will continue until *End-of-job* has been reached. End-of-job will occur when both the input files have no more data to be processed. Since it is not known which file will reach end of file first, the record key of each file will be set to a high value when end of file is reached. When the record key of one of the files is high, the other file will continue to be processed, as required, until the record key on that file is assigned the same high value. End-of-job occurs when the record keys on both the files is the same high value.

Let us now establish a general solution algorithm for a sequential update program. The logic provided will also include the printing of the audit and error reports.

a Hierarchy chart

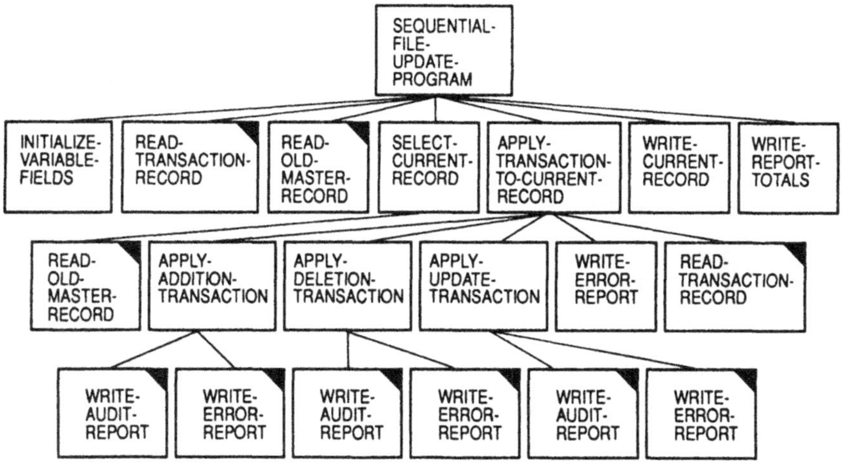

b Solution algorithm

Mainline

```
Sequential-Update-Program
   Initialize-Variable-Fields
   Read-Transaction-Record
   Read-Old-Master-Record
   set current-record-status to 'inactive'
   DOWHILE End-of-Job = false
      Select-Current-Record
      DOWHILE transaction-record-key = current-record-key
         Apply-Transaction-to-Current-Record
      ENDDO
      IF current-record-status = 'active' THEN
         Write-Current-Record
         set current-record-status to 'inactive'
      ENDIF
   ENDDO
   Write-Report-Totals
END
```

Subordinate modules

```
1  Initialize-Variable-Fields
      set total-transaction-recs to zero
      set total-old-master-recs to zero
      set total-new-master-recs to zero
      set total-error-recs to zero
      set End-of-job to false
   END

2  Read-Transaction-Record
      Read transaction record
      IF NOT EOF THEN
         increment total-transaction-recs
      ELSE
         set transaction-record-key to high value
         IF old-master-record-key = high value THEN
            set End-of-job to true
         ENDIF
      ENDIF
   END
```

```
3 Read-Old-Master-Record
     Read old master record
     IF NOT EOF THEN
        increment total-old-master-recs
     ELSE
        set old-master-record-key to high value
        IF transaction-record-key = high value THEN
           set End-of-job = true
        ENDIF
     ENDIF
  END

4 Select-Current-Record
     IF transaction-record-key < old-master-record-key THEN
        set up current record with transaction record fields
     ELSE
        set up current record with old master record fields
        set current-record-status to 'active'
        Read-Old-Master-Record
     ENDIF
  END

5 Apply-Transaction-to-Current-Record
     CASE OF transaction-type
        Addition:  Apply-Addition-Transaction
        Deletion:  Apply-Deletion-Transaction
        Update:    Apply-Update-Transaction
        Other:     Error-message = 'invalid transaction type'
                   Write-Error-Report
     ENDCASE
     Read-Transaction-Record
  END

6 Write-Current-Record
     write current record to new master file
     increment total-new-master-recs
  END

7 Write-Report-Totals
     write total-transaction-recs
     write total-old-master-recs
     write total-new-master-recs
     write total-error-recs
  END
```

```
8 Apply-Addition-Transaction
    IF current-record-status = 'inactive' THEN
        set current-record-status to 'active'
        Write-Audit-Report
    ELSE
        error-message = 'Invalid addition; record already exists'
        Write-Error-Report
    ENDIF
END

9 Apply-Deletion-Transaction
    IF current-record-status = 'active' THEN
        set current-record-status to 'inactive'
        Write-Audit-Report
    ELSE
        error-message = 'Invalid deletion; record not on master file'
        Write-Error-Report
    ENDIF
END

10 Apply-Update-Transaction
    IF current-record-status = 'active' THEN
        apply required change(s) to current record
        Write-Audit-Report
    ELSE
        error-message = 'Invalid update; record not on master file'
        Write-Error-Report
    ENDIF
END

11 Write-Audit-Report
    write transaction details on audit report
    CASE OF transaction-type
        addition  : write 'record added'
        deletion  : write 'record deleted'
        update    : write 'record updated'
    ENDCASE
END

12 Write-Error-Report
    write transaction details on error report
    write error-message
    increment totals-error-recs
END
```

Note that End-of-job is reached when transaction-record-key = high value AND old-master-record-key = high value. This pseudocode algorithm can now be used to process any sequential file update report.

9.6 Array processing

An *array* is a data structure, which is made up of a number of variables which all have the same data type. That is, it is a collection of variables which all look the same; for example, an array of scores, prices or names.

The individual data items which make up the array are referred to as the elements of the array. They are stored in consecutive storage locations, and are assigned a single data name — the name of the array. The individual elements of an array can be distinguished from each other by the use of a subscript or index. The subscript indicates the position of the element within the array; eg scores (3) points to the third element in the array scores.

Arrays are an internal data structure, ie they are required only for the duration of the program in which they are defined. They are a very convenient mechanism for storing and manipulating a collection of similar data items in a program, and a programmer should be familiar with the operations most commonly performed on them.

This section will develop pseudocode algorithms for the most typical operations performed on arrays:

- Reading values into the elements of an array,
- a linear search of an array,
- a binary search of an array, and
- writing out the contents of an array.

1 Reading values into the elements of an array

The reading of a series of values from a file into an array can be represented by a simple DOWHILE loop. The loop should terminate when either:

- the array is full, or
- the input file has reached end of file.

Both these conditions can be catered for in the condition clause of the DOWHILE loop. In the following pseudocode algorithm, the array name is 'array', the subscript 'index', and the value being put into the element of the array is 'input value' . The maximum number of elements which the array can hold is placed in 'max-num-elements'.

```
Read-Values-Into-Array
    set max-num-elements to designated value
    set index to zero
    read first input value
    DOWHILE (input values exist AND
            index < max-num-elements)
        index = index + 1
        array (index) = input value
        read next input value
    ENDDO
END
```

2 A linear search of an array

A common operation on arrays is the searching of the elements of an array for a particular data item. A linear search involves looking at each of the elements of the array, one by one, starting with the first element. The search will continue until:

- the element being looked for is found, or
- the end of the array is reached

The pseudocode algorithm for the linear search of an array will require a program flag named 'Element-found'. This flag, initially set to *false,* will be set to *true* if the current element is the data item which is being looked for. The required data item is stored in the variable 'input-value', and 'max-num-elements' contains the total number of elements in the array.

```
Linear-Search-of-an-Array
    set max-num-elements to designated value
    set Element-found to false
    set index to 1
    DOWHILE (Element-found = false AND
            index < = max-num-elements)
        IF array (index) = input value THEN
            set Element-found to true
        ELSE
            index = index + 1
        ENDIF
    ENDDO
END
```

3 A binary search of an array

When the number of elements in an array exceeds 25, and the elements are ordered into ascending sequence, then a more efficient method of searching the array is a binary search.

A binary search locates the middle element of the array first, and determines if the element being searched for is in the first half or second half of the table. The search then points to the middle element of the relevant half table, and the comparison is then repeated. This technique of continually halving the area under consideration is continued until the data item being searched for is found, or its absence is detected.

In the following algorithm, a program flag named 'Element-found' is used to indicate whether the data item being looked for has been found. 'Low-element' indicates the bottom position of the section of the table being searched, and 'high-element' indicates the top position. The maximum number of elements which the array can hold is placed in 'max-num-elements'.

The binary search will continue until:

- the data item has been found, or
- there can be no more halving operations (ie low-element is not less than high-element).

```
Binary-Search-of-an-Array
    set Element-found to false
    set low-element to 1
    set high-element to max-num-elements
    DOWHILE (Element-found = false AND
                    low-element < = high-element)
        index = (low-element + high-element) / 2
        IF input value = array (index) THEN
            set Element-found to true
        ELSE
            IF input value < array (index) THEN
                high-element = index  – 1
            ELSE
                low-element = index + 1
            ENDIF
        ENDIF
    ENDDO
END
```

4 Writing out the contents of an array

The elements of arrays are often used as accumulators of data, to be written to a report. Writing out the contents of an array can be represented by a simple DOWHILE loop.

In the pseudocode algorithm, the name of the array is 'array', and the subscript is 'index'. The number of elements in the array is represented by 'max-num-elements'.

```
Write-Values-of-Array
   set index to 1
   DOWHILE index < = max-num-elements
      write array (index)
      index = index + 1
   ENDDO
END
```

9.7 Chapter summary

The aim of this chapter was to develop general pseudocode algorithms to five common business applications. The applications covered were:

— report generation with page break,
— single-level control break,
— multiple-level control break,
— sequential file update, and
— array processing

In each section, the application was discussed, a hierarchy chart was developed, and a general solution algorithm was presented in pseudocode. These solution algorithms can be used by beginner programmers when writing programs which incorporate any of the above applications.

9.8 Programming problems

Design a solution algorithm for the following programming problems. Your solution should contain:

- a defining diagram
- a hierarchy chart
- a pseudocode algorithm
- a desk check of the solution

1 Design a program to read the Customer Master File of a clothing manufacturer, and print a report of all the customer records which have an account balance greater than zero.

The Customer Master File contains the customer number, name, address (street, city, state and postcode), and the customer's account balance.

The output report must show all the customers' details, and three total lines as indicated. There are to be 35 detail lines per page.

GLAD RAGS CLOTHING COMPANY

xx/xx/xx	CURRENT ACCOUNT BALANCES		PAGE xx
CUSTOMER NUMBER	CUSTOMER NAME	CUSTOMER ADDRESS	ACCOUNT BALANCE
xxxxx	xxxxxxxxxx	xxxxxxxxxxxxxxxxxxxx	9 999.99
xxxxx	xxxxxxxxxx	xxxxxxxxxxxxxxxxxxxx	9 999.99
		TOTAL CUSTOMERS ON FILE	999
		TOTAL CUSTOMERS WITH BALANCE OWING	999
		TOTAL BALANCE OWING	99 999.99

2 Design a program which will read the Sales File for the Multi-Disk Computer Company, and produce a Sales Report by salesperson. The Sales Report shows the details of each sale made per salesperson, and a total of the sales for that salesperson.

The fields on the Sales File are the salesperson's number and name, the product number of the product sold, the quantity sold and the price of the product. There may be many records for each salesperson, depending on the products sold that month. The Sales File has been sorted into ascending sequence of salesperson number.

Your program is to read the Sales File sequentially, calculate the extension amount (price * quantity sold) for each product sold and print a detail line for each record processed. Control total lines showing the sales total for each salesperson are to be printed on change of salesperson number.

The report details are to be printed, as per the 'Sales Report by Salesperson' report shown overleaf.

MULTI-DISK COMPUTER COMPANY

xx/xx/xx	SALES REPORT BY SALESPERSON				PAGE xx
SALESPERSON NUMBER	SALESPERSON NAME	PRODUCT NUMBER	QTY SOLD	PRICE	EXTENSION AMOUNT
xxxx	xxxxxxxxxx	xxxx	99	999.99	9 999.99
		xxxx	99	999.99	9 999.99
		xxxx	99	999.99	9 999.99
		SALES TOTAL FOR xxxxxxxxxx			99 999.99
		REPORT SALES TOTAL			999 999.99

3 The same Sales File as described in Problem 2 exists, with the addition of a further field, department number. The Sales File has been sorted into ascending sequence of salesperson number within department number. The same Sales Report is to be printed, with the additional requirement of a sales total on change of department number, as well as salesperson number.

The report details are to be printed as per the 'Sales Report' shown below:

MULTI-DISK COMPUTER COMPANY

xx/xx/xx		SALES REPORT				PAGE xx
DEPT	SALESPERSON NUMBER	SALESPERSON NAME	PRODUCT NUMBER	QTY SOLD	PRICE	EXTENSION AMOUNT
xx	xxxx	xxxxxxxxxx	xxxx	99	999.99	9 999.99
			xxxx	99	999.99	9 999.99
			xxxx	99	999.99	9 999.99
		SALES TOTAL FOR xxxxxxxxxx				99 999.99
		SALES TOTAL FOR DEPT xx				999 999.99
		REPORT SALES TOTAL				9999 999.99

4 The Yummy Chocolates Confectionery Company requires a program to sequentially update its Customer Master File. A sequential file of update transactions is to be used as the input file, along with the Customer Master file.

The Customer Master File contains the customer number, customer name, customer address (street, city, state and postcode) and account balance. The Customer Transaction File contains the same fields, as well as a transaction code of 'A' (add), 'D' (delete) and 'U' (update).

Both files have been sorted into customer number sequence. There can be multiple update transactions for any one Customer Master record. A new Customer Master File is created.

Transaction records are to be processed as follows:

1 If the transaction record is an 'Add', then the transaction is to be written to the New Customer Master File.
2 If the transaction record is a 'Delete' then the Old Master Record with the same customer number is not to be written to the New Customer Master File.
3 If the transaction record is an update then the Old Master Record with the same customer number is to be updated as follows:

— if customer name is present, update customer name;
— if street is present, update street
— if town is present, update town
— if state is present, update state
— if postcode is present, update postcode
— if balance paid is present, then subtract balance paid from account balance on old customer master record.

As each transaction is processed, then the transaction details are to be printed on the Customer Master Audit Report, with the message, 'record added', 'record deleted' or 'record updated' as applicable.

If a transaction record is in error then the transaction details are to be printed on the Customer Update Errors Report, with one of the following messages:

— 'invalid addition, customer already exists'
— 'invalid deletion, customer not on file'
— 'invalid update, customer not on file'.

5 A program is required to validate the product code on a Product Transaction File. A file of valid product codes is to be read into an array at the beginning of the program. There can be up to 300 products at any time.

Once the product codes have been set up in the array, the Product Transaction file is to be read sequentially. The product code on each transaction record is to be validated by searching the array for that product code. If the search is successful, then no further action is to take place. If the product code is not found in the array, then the transaction record is to be written to the Transaction Errors Report, with the message 'invalid transaction code'. Totals at the end of the report should include the total number of valid transactions, and the total number of invalid transactions.

CHAPTER 10

CONCLUSION

Objective

- Revision of the steps required to achieve 'good' program design

Outline

10.1 Simple program design

The aim of this textbook has been to encourage learner programmers to follow a series of simple steps in order to develop solution algorithms to given programming problems.

1 Step one is *define the problem*. To do this, the programmer should underline the nouns and verbs in the problem description. This helps to divide the problem into its input, output and processing components. These components can be represented in a defining diagram — a table which lists the input to the problem, the expected output, and the processing steps required to produce this output.

   The programmer at this stage should only be concerned with *what* needs to be done. So, when writing down the *processing* component, the programmer should simply list the activities to be performed without being concerned about *how* to perform them.

2 Secondly, *group the activities into subtasks or functions*. To do this, the programmer should look at the defining diagram and group the activities in the *processing* component into separate tasks. There are often several activities listed in the processing component which all contribute to the performance of a single task. These separate tasks are called functions. By grouping the activities together to form subtasks, the programmer is establishing the major functions of the problem.

   It should be noted that not all the activities to be performed may have been listed in the defining diagram. If the problem is large, only the top-level subtasks may have been identified at this stage. The basic aim of top-down development is to develop the higher-level modules first and to only develop the lower-level modules once the higher-level modules have been established. The programmer should concentrate on these higher-level functions, before attempting to consider further subordinate functions.

3 The third step is the construction of a *hierarchy chart*. To do this, the programmer should study the defining diagram, which now has the major tasks identified on it, and illustrate these tasks or functions on a hierarchy chart. The functions identified on the hierarchy chart will become the future modules of the program.

   The hierarchy chart not only shows the modules of the program, but also their relationship to each other, in similar fashion to the organizational chart of a large company.

   Just as a company director can change the organization of his or her company to suit its operation so a programmer can change the organization of the modules in the hierarchy chart. It is good programming practice to study the way the modules have been organized in the overall structure of the program, and to attempt to make this structure as simple and *top-down* as possible.

Note that the programmer is still only concerned with *what* tasks are to be performed. Once the hierarchical structure of the algorithm has been developed, the programmer can begin to consider the logic of the solution.

4 The fourth step is to *establish the logic of the mainline of the algorithm.* The programmer can use pseudocode and the three basic control structures to establish this logic. Pseudocode is a subset of English which has been formalized and abbreviated to look like a high level computer language. Keywords and indentation are used to signify particular control structures. The three basic control structures are simple sequence, selection and repetition.

Because the programmer has already identified the major functions of the problem, he or she can now use pseudocode and the three control structures to develop the mainline logic. This mainline should show the main processing functions of the problem and the order in which they are to be performed.

In this text, you were shown that the mainline for most algorithms which process a sequential file follow the same basic pattern. This pattern contains some initial processing before the loop, some processing of the record within the loop, and some final processing after exiting the loop.

Chapter 9 developed a general pseudocode algorithm for five common business applications. These algorithms were for the generation of a report with a page break, a single-level control break program, a multiple-level control break program, a sequential file update program and some algorithms used in the processing of arrays. The algorithms which were developed have good program structure, and high modular.cohesion, and it is recommended that programmers use these algorithms for their specific programming problems.

5 The fifth step involves the development of the *pseudocode for each successive module in the hierarchy chart.* The algorithms for these modules should be developed in a top-down fashion. That is, the pseudocode for each module on the first level should be established, before attempting the pseudocode for the modules on the next or lower level. The modularization process is complete when the pseudocode for each module on the lowest level of the hierarchy chart has been developed.

6 The final step is to *desk check the solution algorithm*. By desk checking the algorithm, you attempt to find any logic errors which have crept into the solution.

Desk checking involves tracing through the logic of the algorithm with some chosen test data exactly as the computer would operate. The programmer keeps track of all variable values in a table as the algorithm is *walked through*. At the end, the programmer checks that the output expected from the test data matches the output developed in the desk check.

This detection of errors, early in the design process, can save many frustrating hours during the testing phase. This is because the programmer assumes that the logic of the algorithm is correct, when he or she begins coding. Then, when errors occur, the programmer usually concentrates on the individual lines of code, rather than the initial logic expressed in the algorithm.

It is essential that the programmer desk checks the solution algorithm, and yet this step is so often avoided. Most programmers bypass this step because they either assume the algorithm is correct, or because they believe desk checking is not creative. While it may not be as stimulating as the original design phase, it is really just as satisfying to know that the logic is correct.

10.2 Chapter summary

This chapter has revised the steps required for a programmer to achieve *good* program design. Program design is considered *good* if it is easy to read and understand and easy to alter.

If a programmer follows these six steps in the development of an algorithm he or she will rapidly achieve a high level of competence.

APPENDIX

This appendix contains a number of algorithms which are not included in the body of the textbook and yet may be required at some time in a programmer's career.

The first three algorithms are sorting algorithms, viz bubble sort, insertion sort and selection sort. Then follow five algorithms which manipulate the elements of an array.

1 Sorting algorithms

1.1 Bubble sort algorithm

This algorithm sorts an integer array into ascending order using a bubble sort method.

The algorithm, on each pass, compares each pair of adjacent items in the array. If the pair is out of order they are switched, otherwise they will remain in the original order.

As a result, at the end of the first pass, the largest element in the array will have *bubbled* to the last position in the array.

The next pass will work only with the remaining elements, and will move the next largest element to the second-last position in the array and so on.

In the algorithm:

```
I = index for outer loop
J = index for inner loop
Elements-switched = flag to record if a switch of elements has
                    been made in the current pass
Temp = temporary area for holding an array element which is
       being switched
ARRAY = array to be sorted
Number-of-elements = number of elements in the array
```

It is assumed that the contents of the ARRAY and the Number-of-elements have already been established.

Bubble-sort-algorithm

```
   set I to Number-of-elements
   set Elements-switched = true
   DOWHILE (I > = 2 AND Elements-switched = true)
      set J to 1
      set Elements-switched to false
      DOWHILE J < = I – 1
         IF ARRAY (J) > ARRAY (J + 1) THEN
            Temp = ARRAY (J)
            ARRAY (J) = ARRAY (J + 1)
            ARRAY (J + 1) = Temp
            Elements-switched = true
         ENDIF
         J = J + 1
      ENDDO
      I = I – 1
   ENDDO
END
```

1.2 Insertion sort algorithm

This algorithm sorts an integer array into ascending order, using an insertion sort method.

In the algorithm, the array is scanned until an out-of-order element is found. The scan is then temporarily halted while a backward scan is made to find the correct position to insert the out-of-order element. Elements bypassed during this backward scan are moved up one position to make room for the element being inserted.

This method of sorting is more efficient than the bubble sort.

In the algorithm:

I = current position of the element
J = index for inner loop
Temp = temporary area for holding an array element while correct position is being searched
ARRAY = array to be sorted
Number-of-elements = number of elements in the array

It is assumed that the contents of the ARRAY and the Number-of-elements have been established.

```
Insertion-sort-algorithm
   set I to 1
   DOWHILE I < = Number-of-elements – 1
      IF ARRAY (I) > ARRAY (I + 1) THEN
         Temp = ARRAY (I + 1)
         J = I
         DOWHILE (J > = 1 AND ARRAY (J) > Temp)
            ARRAY (J + 1) = ARRAY (J)
            J = J – 1
         ENDDO
         ARRAY (J + 1) = Temp
      ENDIF
      I = I + 1
   ENDDO
END
```

1.3 Selection sort algorithm

This algorithm sorts an integer array into ascending sequence using a selection sort method.

The algorithm on the first pass will find the smallest element in the array and move it to the first position in the array by switching it with the element originally in that position. Each successive pass moves one more element into position. After the number of passes is one number less than the number of elements in the array, the array will be in order.

This method of sorting is less efficient than the bubble sort.

In the algorithm:

```
I  = index for outer loop
J  = index for inner loop
Smallest-element  =  area for holding the smallest element found
                     in that pass
Current-smallest-position  =  contains the value of the current
                              position to place the smallest
                              element
ARRAY = array being sorted
Number-of-elements = number of elements in the array
```

It is assumed that the contents of the ARRAY and the Number-of-elements have been established.

Selection-sort-algorithm

```
   Set Current-smallest-position to 1
   DOWHILE Current-smallest-position < = Number-of-elements – 1
      Set I to Current-smallest-position
      Smallest-element = ARRAY (I)
      Set J = I + 1
      DOWHILE J < = Number-of-elements
         IF ARRAY (J) < Smallest-element THEN
            I = J
            Smallest-element = ARRAY (J)
         ENDIF
         J = J + 1
      ENDDO
      ARRAY (I) = ARRAY (Current-smallest-position)
      ARRAY (Current-smallest-position) = Smallest-element
      Add 1 to Current-smallest-position
   ENDDO
END
```

2 Algorithms which manipulate arrays

The following algorithms involve the manipulation of arrays. It is assumed that the contents of the ARRAY, and the Number-of-elements have been established.

2.1 Find the sum of the elements of an array

```
Calculate-sum-of-elements
   set Sum to zero
   set I to 1
   DOWHILE I < = Number-of-elements
      Sum = Sum + ARRAY (I)
      I = I + 1
   ENDDO
   Print Sum
END
```

2.2 Find the largest of the elements of an array

```
Find-largest-element
   set I to 1
   set Largest-element to ARRAY (I)
   DOWHILE I < Number-of-elements
      IF ARRAY (I + 1) > Largest-element THEN
         Largest-element = ARRAY (I + 1)
      ENDIF
      I = I + 1
   ENDDO
   Print Largest-element
END
```

2.3 Find the smallest of the elements of an array

```
Find-smallest-element
   set I to 1
   set Smallest-element to ARRAY (I)
   DOWHILE I < Number-of-elements
      IF ARRAY (I + 1) < Smallest-element THEN
         Smallest-element = ARRAY (I + 1)
      ENDIF
      I = I + 1
   ENDDO
   Print Smallest-element
END
```

2.4 Find the range of the elements of an array

```
Find-range-of-elements
   set I to 1
   set Smallest-element to ARRAY (I)
   set Largest-element to ARRAY (I)
   DOWHILE I < Number-of-elements
      IF ARRAY (I + 1) < Smallest-element THEN
         Smallest-element = ARRAY (I + 1)
      ELSE
         IF ARRAY (I + 1) > Largest-element THEN
            Largest-element = ARRAY (I + 1)
         ENDIF
      ENDIF
      I = I + 1
   ENDDO
   Print the range as Smallest-element followed by Largest-Element
END
```

2.5 Find the mean of the elements of an array

```
Find-mean-of-elements
   set I to 1
   set Sum to zero
   DOWHILE I < = Number-of-elements
      Sum = Sum + ARRAY (I)
      I = I + 1
   ENDDO
   Mean = Sum / Number-of-elements
   Print Mean
END
```

GLOSSARY

algorithm An algorithm is a set of detailed, unambiguous and ordered instructions developed to describe the processes necessary to produce the desired output from the given input.

array A data structure which is made up of a number of variables which all have the same type.

CASE control structure This structure extends the basic selection control structure from a choice between two values to a choice from multiple values.

cohesion A measure of the internal strength of a module ie how closely the elements or statements of a module are associated with each other. The higher the cohesion, the better the module.

control structures The Structure Theorem states that it is possible to write any program using only three basic control structures:

(i) sequence: the straightforward execution of one processing step after another.

(ii) selection: the presentation of a condition, and the choice between two actions, depending on whether the condition is true or false.

(iii) repetition: the presentation of a set of instructions to be performed repeatedly, as long as a condition is true.

coupling A measure of the extent of information interchange between modules. The fewer the connections between modules, the more loosely they are coupled. The looser the coupling, the better the module.

defining diagram This diagram arranges the input, output and processing components of a problem into separate columns. It is constructed when the programmer defines the problem.

file A collection of records.

global data Data which is known to the *whole world* of the program.

hierarchy chart Shows the name of each module in the solution algorithm and its hierarchical relationship to the other modules.

inter-module communication Refers to the flow of information or data between modules.

local data Local data is data which is defined within the module in which it will be referenced. This data will not be known ouside that module.

mainline The mainline is the controlling module of a solution algorithm, which ties all the modules together and co-ordinates their activity.

modular design Modular design involves the grouping of tasks together because they all perform the same function. Modular design is directly connected to top-down development as the tasks which the programmer breaks the problem into will actually form the future modules of the program.

module A section of an algorithm which is dedicated to the performance of a single task.

parameter A variable, literal or constant, which can communicate between the modules of a program.

- *Data parameters* contain the actual variables or data items which will be passed between modules.
- *Status parameters* act as program flags and should contain just one of two values, *true* or *false.*

priming read A statement which appears immediately before the DOWHILE condition in a solution algorithm.

pseudocode A subset of English which has been formalized and abbreviated to look like a high level computer language. Keywords and indentation are used to signify particular control structures.

record A collection of fields which all bear some relationship to each other.

scope of a variable The list of all the modules in which that variable could be referenced.

sentinel A special record placed at the end of valid data to signify the end of that data. It is also known as a trailer record.

side effect This occurs when a subordinate module alters the value of a global variable.

Structure Theorem The Structure Theorem states that it is possible to write any computer program by using only three basic control structures. These control structures are simple sequence, selection and repetition.

structured programming This is the method of writing programs so that each instruction obeys the Structure Theorem. Structured programming also incorporates top-down development and modular design.

top-down development Refers to the breaking of a problem into separate tasks before the programmer begins to consider the solution algorithm. The programmer develops an algorithm which incorporates the major tasks first and only considers the more detailed steps when all the major tasks have been completed.

INDEX

Printed in France by Amazon
Brétigny-sur-Orge, FR

51786476R00107